CREATING
Beautiful Boxes WITH
Inlay Techniques

DOUG STOWE

POPULAR WOODWORKING BOOKS

CINCINNATI, OHIO

DISCLAIMER The author and editors who compiled this book have tried to make all the contents as accurate and as correct as possible. Plans, illustrations, photographs and text have been carefully checked. All instructions, plans and projects should be carefully read, studied and understood before beginning construction. Due to the variability of local conditions, construction materials, skill levels, etc., neither the authors, nor Betterway Books, assumes any responsibility for any accidents, injuries, damages or other losses incurred resulting from the material presented in this book.

SAFETY FIRST! To prevent accidents, keep safety in mind while you work. Use the safety guards installed on power equipment; they are for your protection. When working on power equipment, keep fingers away from saw blades, wear safety goggles to prevent injuries from flying wood chips and sawdust, and wear headphones to protect your hearing.

METRIC CONVERSION CHART

TO CONVERT	TO	MULTIPLY BY
Inches	Centimeters	2.54
Centimeters	Inches	0.4

Visit our website at www.popularwoodworking.com for information on more resources for woodworkers.

10 09 08 07 06   12 11 10 9 8

Library of Congress Cataloging-in-Publication Data

Stowe, Doug.
    Creating beautiful boxes with inlay techniques / by Doug Stowe.
        p.   cm.
    Includes index.
    ISBN-13: 978-1-55870-443-5 (pbk: alk. paper)
    ISBN-10: 1-55870-443-4 (pbk: alk. paper)
    1. Marquetry. 2. Box making. 3. Wooden boxes. I. Title.
TT192.S76   1997
745.51′2—dc21

97-18861
CIP

Editor: R. Adam Blake
Production editor: Bob Beckstead
Designer: Brian Roeth
Cover photo: Pamela Monfort Braun/Bronze Photography

To Douglas R. Stowe, Sr., and the encouragement that fathers give their sons and daughters.

ACKNOWLEDGMENTS

My thanks to:

Jean and Lucy, for their enthusiastic support.

Dorothy Stowe, my Mom. If creativity is genetic, I know where I got mine.

Adam Blake, editor, for his encouragement to let this book grow beyond what was planned for it.

Joseph W. Bradley for creating the drawings of the boxes in this book.

The staff at Betterway Books.

Bob Jeffreys.

The artist community of Eureka Springs.

Cliff Paddock, Jesada Tools.

Pete Spooler and Coleman Forshay, Klingspors' Sanding Catalog.

Jon Behrle, Woodcraft Supply.

My customers—friends who have challenged and trusted me to transcend my limitations.

Claude Nations for introducing me to our native woods.

Guy Loyd for teaching me the basics of meditation.

ABOUT THE AUTHOR

Doug Stowe is a professional furniture designer/craftsman and box maker. He lives with his wife, Jean, and daughter, Lucy, on a wooded hillside overlooking the town of Eureka Springs, Arkansas.

His boxes have been carried around the world as gifts by the governors of Arkansas, and are available for purchase in galleries throughout the United States. His furniture has been featured in *Woodworker's Journal* and *Fine Woodworking*.

Portrait by Bob Jeffreys

TABLE OF CONTENTS

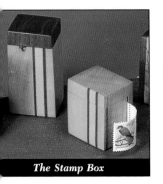
The Stamp Box

The Art of Inlay

The Koa Box

The Pen Box

A Simple Inlaid Box

The Triangle Box

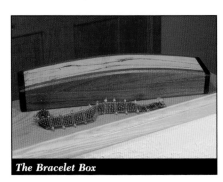
The Bracelet Box

The Walnut Box

Introduction   6

CD Cabinet

The Tea Chest

The Checkerboard Inlay Box

Sculpted Pecan Box

Earring and Pin Chest

Fiddleback Maple Jewelry Chest

Jewelry Box With Dovetails

Rachel's Jewelry Cabinet

It is ironic for me to be offering plans and detailed step-by-step instructions for making the boxes and small cabinets in this book. I am a "seat of the pants" woodworker, meaning that I embark on most projects with very few of the details worked out in advance. Most of my projects start out as very simple concept sketches, often drawn at the end of a board, or on whatever scrap of wood or paper I have at hand. I sometimes stand with my hands and arms forming the shape of a piece while my imagination fills in the blanks.

My daughter, Lucy, observed recently while watching me in the shop, "Daddy, you doodle on everything." And it's true. I draw much of my inspiration from the woods I use, and the inspiration for my projects is much more likely to come as I look through my stacks of lumber than at the drawing board. So while many woodworkers start out with full-scale, highly detailed drawings, I like to leave a lot of loose ends in my designs. I like to let the lumber at hand and its figure say something about the proportions of a piece. It works for me, and it allows the unique character within the wood greater opportunity to be better expressed.

I suppose it's a left brain, right brain thing. With the left brain planning, comparing, concerned with proper technique, I often leave it out of the process until it's needed, occasionally until it's too late. The right brain seems to be where I am most at home, viewing life as art, dawdling, savoring the moment, going with the flow, working out the small details of a project when they become clear, sketching on a Post-it or scratch pad for confirmation, and then cutting the wood. Surprisingly, I am able to work without keeping a lot of it in my head. The pieces of a project have their own memory, and a glance can tell me where I left off when I quit yesterday evening and what must still be done.

Over twenty years ago, I read James Krenov's *Cabinet Maker's Notebook*, and realized that a person's work with wood and an underlying commitment to growth, mindfulness and quality could give meaning to one's life. I am grateful to his example and the challenge offered.

I wouldn't be a woodworker today without the encouragement of my father, Douglas R. Stowe, Sr. Some of my earliest memories are of his instructions in how to hold a hammer so as not to hit my thumb as I "helped" in the remodeling of our family home in Memphis, Tennessee. I enjoyed many Saturday trips to the "lumma lard" to buy nails and lumber for various projects. For my fourteenth birthday, he gave me an old, used 1948 Model 10 ER Shop Smith, which I use regularly in my present shop. So you can see that, as a woodworker, I started out standing on my father's shoulders. I am telling all this because I believe woodworking is about values, and the search for deeper meaning in our lives.

I am deeply grateful to my wife, Jean, and daughter, Lucy, for their encouragement of my work and their patience with me while writing this book. I am grateful to live in Eureka Springs, Arkansas, a small community in which there are more artists than attorneys, CPAs, bankers and brokers combined. I could not do what I do without their companionship, example and encouragement.

I remind my readers that copyright laws are written to protect artists from being copied in the marketplace, and that my sharing the designs and techniques used in my work does not grant license to produce these pieces for sale.

There is a saying that the teacher's work is completed when his students surpass him. Some of you will accept the challenge and opportunity that wood offers of reaching toward excellence, growth and personal expression. It is you for whom I write in the knowledge that you will surpass me.

CHAPTER I

A Simple Inlaid Box

A simple inlaid box was one of my first commercial products. Designed for a jeweler in my home-town to use as presentation boxes to be sold with his jewelry, I made them in a variety of shapes and sizes for rings, necklaces and bracelets. His customers became interested in them and asked to purchase them without jewelry, so I was immediately in the box business, and made hundreds in this design over a period of several years. I found box making to be a great supplement to my woodworking business, keeping me busy between fur-niture commissions.

This box body is made without mechanical fasteners and relies only on the glued joint holding the ends to the top and sides, which are cut from a single piece of wood. This is not the ideal way to join wood (given its tendency to expand and contract) and one would certainly have greater difficulties with this design if it were made larger. Perhaps it was beginner's luck that has held so many of them together for twenty years, but I have several of them around that still show no sign of coming apart, and often find them on the coffee tables of old friends. I present this technique because it was the start of my own box-building adventure.

My first step in making this box was to edge join ⅞″ walnut stock long enough to make the tops and bottoms of the planned boxes, then rip it about ¹⁄₁₆″ oversize and pass it through the planer at 3″ to attain the desired width. To make a box with a 7″ inside length (long enough to hold pens, but not pencils), I used a piece of walnut 14½″ long.

MAKING THE PATTERNED INLAY

I began making this type of inlay a very short time after I began my woodworking career. I have continued to refine and use this technique for twenty years, because it is a simple way to share my interest in the variety of North American hardwoods and help people to better understand the wealth of our forests. I start with 1"-thick pieces of wood from several species. Some of my favorites for use in inlay are walnut, cherry, elm, sassafras, maple, persimmon, honey locust and ash. I like to use woods that contrast in texture and grain as well as color, and while these woods could be cut into much smaller pieces, making the inlay much more intricate, it is important to me that enough of the natural characteristics of each wood is allowed to remain that someone can say, "So, *that's* what sassafras looks like."

STEP 1
Cut Stock Into 1" Strips
Taking the 1"-thick pieces of various hardwoods, join one side flat and one edge straight and square, and then rip the pieces to a uniform width, about twice the width of the planned inlay, on the table saw.

STEP 2
Cut to Length
Next, cut the pieces into lengths about ⅝" long, using a cutoff box on the table saw.

STEP 3
Glue-Up Strips
Next, arrange the pieces of the various woods in a pattern as in the photo below, with the pieces lined up end grain to end grain. After you have arranged your pattern, apply glue to each piece. Because you are gluing end grain, apply plenty of glue to both parts. As they are glued, place them back in the arranged order. In order to work with a safe cutting length on the table saw, I usually glue up lengths from about 18" to 36", arranging them along a piece of scrap wood ½" shorter than the length of the pieces. After glue is applied to all the pieces except the end pieces, use a bar clamp to pull the pieces tight. Always be careful, at

MATERIALS LIST		
Brass hinges	1 pr.	1" × 13⁄16" open
Top and bottom	2 pcs.	7⁄8" × 3" × 6¾"
Ends	4 pcs.	5⁄16" × 15⁄16" × 3⅛"
4/4 Cherry, sassafras, ash, walnut and maple		3" × 6"
Strips of walnut	2 pcs.	⅛" × 1" (for inlay borders)

TOOLS LIST	
Table saw	Jointer
Planer	Bar clamps
Belt or disc sander	Router table
1" straight-cut router bit	

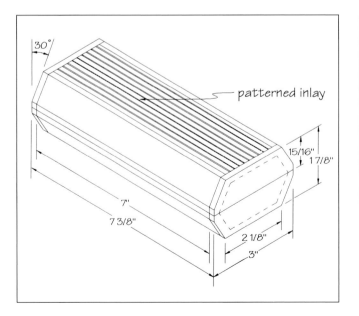

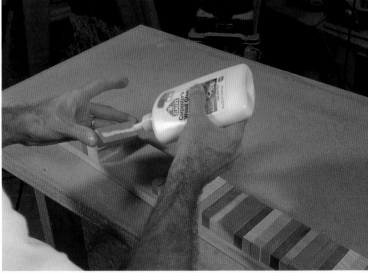

Apply plenty of glue when joining end grain. Lay the pattern out dry first and follow the same arrangement as the glue is applied.

this point, to make sure that all of the pieces have stayed in place. They usually move around a bit as the clamp applies pressure, so chase them back in place. When you are satisfied that the pieces are being glued up where you want them, lift the clamped and glued pieces off the piece of scrap wood and set them aside to dry. If the glued-up block shows any sign of bending toward or away from the bar clamp, insert shims between the block and the bar, or use a C-clamp to pull the block closer to the bar. Being certain the glued-up inlay block is flat will ensure that you are able to get the maximum number of inlay strips from the block. After the glue is dry, remove the clamp, and joint one face and one edge flat on the jointer.

STEP 4
Rip the Inlay Into Thin Strips
Using a sharp thin-kerf carbide blade in the table saw, begin ripping thin strips from the block glued-up from the hardwood pieces. I usually rip the first strips thicker, and work my way down to the thinner strips. Ripping thin strips on the table saw is a delicate and dangerous operation that calls for the use of push blocks and requires a zero-clearance table saw blade insert to give the strips firm support and keep them from chattering and bouncing. Rather than risk injury, always plan the glued-up block to be wide enough to allow for some waste.

STEP 5
Make the Inlay Border
Next, rip walnut into thin strips, about ⅛″ × 1″, that will be used as the border strips to surround the pattern.

STEP 6
Arrange the Inlay Pattern
After the strips are cut from the patterned block, rearrange them in relation to each other, sliding them into a visually pleasing pattern. When you have the pattern you want, mark across it with a pencil, so that as the slices are glued you will know how to place them back in the desired relationship. Apply glue to one of the walnut border strips, then to each strip in succession, and finish with the other border strip. Be careful to make sure that each strip is laid down in its exact position before the next one is laid down. In a wide pattern, the bottom strips can be starting to get a good glue grip by the time the second border strip goes on. Use blocks of hardwood on both sides of the strip when it is being clamped. This ensures good distribution of clamping pressure and helps the strips to come out straight. I usually use several bar clamps along the length of the strip and apply a lot of pressure to make sure the

After the glue is dry, joint one edge 90° to the face.

Begin ripping thin strips from the block glued-up from the hardwood pieces. Make sure you put the flat face on the table and your 90° edge on the fence.

Rearrange the strips into a visually pleasing pattern and glue them together. The trick here is to maintain symmetry and smooth movement within the pattern.

Use blocks of hardwood on both sides of the strip when it is being clamped to ensure both good distribution of clamping pressure and that the finished strips come out straight.

strips get a good grip with each other. By this time, I'm usually ready to let the patterned blocks sit overnight before releasing the clamps.

STEP 7

Rip the Pattern Strips

After releasing the clamps join the face flat and begin ripping thin patterned strips on the table saw. Use the thin-kerf blade, the zero-clearance insert and a push stick for safety when ripping thin strips. The very last strip takes special care since it is so thin and so close to the saw blade. Use a push block for this final cut to keep your hands safe.

INLAYING THE TOP

STEP 1

Inlay the Top

Inlay the top before the shape is cut in the box because it is easiest to clamp the inlay in place during gluing while the top is still a squared block of solid wood. Mounting a 1″ straight-cut router bit in the router table, set the height of cut to just under the thickness of my finished inlay strips. Set the fence on the router table to cut 1″-wide channels where you want the inlay strips to fit. The finished inlay strip I made for this use is about 1½″ wide before joining and sizing, so I cut the channel wider with a second pass, widening the distance between the bit and the fence to its finished width of 1⅜″. Make the first cut moving the workpiece along the fence as shown right, center, and widen the channel by adjusting the fence and moving the workpiece in the opposite direction to make the second cut. This technique avoids a climb cut, which can grab the workpiece and pull fingers into the moving bit in the router table.

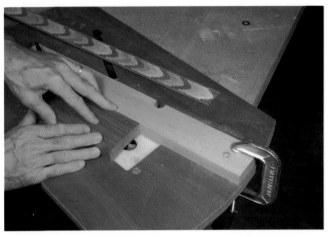

Using the router table, inlay the top before the shape is cut. Set the height of cut to just under the thickness of the finished inlay strips. This will give you room to sand the installed inlay flush with the top. Set the fence on the router table to cut 1″-channels the width of the inlay strips.

Make the first cut moving the workpiece along the fence as shown, and the second cut to widen the channel by adjusting the fence and moving the workpiece in the opposite direction.

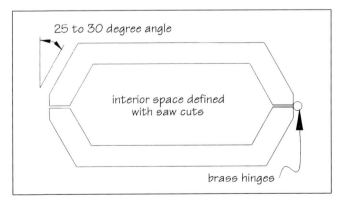

25 to 30 degree angle

interior space defined with saw cuts

brass hinges

The final fitting is done on the router table. To avoid the danger of climb-feeding on the router table, pass the inlay pieces from left to right between the fence and the router bit.

A guard placed over the router bit helps to make this a safe cut.

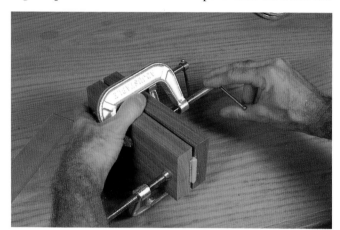

Spread the glue evenly inside the channel to prevent squeeze-out on the top of the box.

Press the inlay strips in place and clamp them with a backing strip thick enough to evenly distribute the clamping pressure.

STEP 2

Size the Inlay

After the channel is cut to about ⅛″ narrower than the inlay strip, size the strips by first cutting them the length of the wood to be inlaid, and then passing one edge across the jointer to make it flat. Try to take enough off with the jointer so that, when the strip is finish-fitted, the border around the pattern will be approximately even on both sides. The final fitting is done on the router table. Raise the 1″ cutter up above the thickness of the inlay, and set the width between the cutter and the fence equal to the width of the channel. Follow a trial-and-error procedure in this: Using a test strip made from scrap, cut the strip a bit too wide at first and move the fence in closer to get a good fit. When the scrap piece fits snug, with no spaces on either side, and is not too difficult to set in place, cut the inlay strips to size.

STEP 3

Trim and Install the Inlay

To avoid the danger of climb-feeding on the router table, pass the inlay pieces from left to right between the fence and the router bit, against the direction of the cutter. Use a push stick to keep your fingers safe, and place a guard over the router bit for additional safety. Apply glue to the

inside of the routed channel, spread it evenly with your fingers, and then press the inlay strips in place and clamp them with a backing strip thick enough to evenly distribute the clamping pressure. Use C-clamps for this job.

FORMING THE INSIDE OF THE BOX

STEP 1

Make 90° Cuts on the Table Saw

Form the inside of the box by making repetitive saw cuts, the kerf of each cut adding to the space within the box. Use a blade that leaves a V-shaped crown. Be careful to adjust the fence for each cut so the repeating kerfs form a delicate pattern on the bottom surface of the inside of the box. Many customers comment positively about this unique feature, which would be lost if care was not taken in setting up the fence and the surface became rough and unattractive. Make the initial cuts with the blade set at 90° on the table saw, positioning the first cut at the exact center, moving the fence away from the blade just under the width of the kerf, turning the workpiece end for end to cut on both sides, and making these cuts until the opening is 1¾″ wide.

TOOLS

My first tool was an old used Shop Smith that my father gave me as a birthday present in 1962. My Shop Smith and I are both 1948 vintage. The nearly half-century-old tool works better now than it did when I first got it—I suspect that my years of almost daily use have finally broken it in. Like most woodworkers that have been doing it for some time, I have gradually accumulated a shop full of tools and have the dilemma of "where would I put that?", if I were to add anything new. So I am very careful in making decisions about buying tools. Actually, some of the best tools for me have been the ones I've figured out how to do without. There is a Zen saying that "Poverty is your greatest treasure, never trade it for an easy life." There is a very strong temptation to fill our shops with wonderful gadgets that take the risk and the opportunities for "failure" and growth out of our lives. One unfortunate factor in all this is that every tool leaves its mark, and with a world full of woodworkers, all using the newest and latest, our work can all start to look alike. From the hand chisel to the computerized milling machine, each tool gives its signature to the finished piece, that is apparent either in the finished surfaces, or in the design accommodations made to allow its use. I have been learning to be very careful about acquiring tools. At one time, I learned to do without the newest and latest tools because I couldn't afford them. I have since learned that the uniqueness of what I do is there in part because, by not being able to afford them, I have figured out my own ways to do my work. And while I doubt that the techniques I work with are unique, I get some personal satisfaction from having discovered them for myself.

It takes a great deal of time to exhaust the possible uses of any given tool, and it takes time and use to develop a skilled relationship with it. Having too much to relate to by having too many tools in the shop, can deprive a beginner of the opportunity to develop meaningful relationships with any of his or her tools, and even cause one to get locked up in indecision over whether to use this tool, or that, when either would do the job.

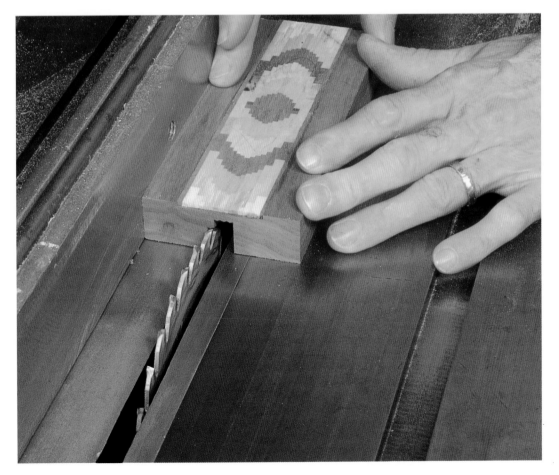

The first cut on the inside of the box should be right in the middle.

With the angle of the blade at 35°, cut away the final sections to form the hollow of the box.

Raise the blade height to just over the full thickness of the workpiece and reset the fence to shape the outside of the box.

STEP 2
Make the Angle Cuts
Change the angle of the blade to about 30° from perpendicular, and raise it so that it cuts at the same height as the cuts made at 90°. Adjust the fence so that the blade cuts the final section away to form the hollow of the box.

STEP 3
Cut Off the Sides
With the blade set at the same angle, raise the blade height to just over the full thickness of the workpiece and set the fence to cut the matching angle on the outside of the box.

ASSEMBLING THE BOX

Now that the interior shape of the box is defined, the next job is to cut the shaped box bodies to length and glue on the end pieces. The ends, made of walnut, are from stock resawn on the table saw and planed to dimension. Each box requires four end pieces, which are made oversize in length and width to allow for inaccuracies in clamping and gluing the pieces in place.

STEP 1
Cut the Parts to Size
Using the cutoff box on the table saw, cut the box bodies to the length desired, and then cut the end pieces to the finished length.

STEP 2
Attach the End Pieces
Assemble the boxes by applying glue to the ends of the box bodies and then placing the end pieces in position. Use a flat scrap board to build a row of the tops and bottoms together, and then use a bar clamp and end blocks to pull the joints tight. Immediately and carefully check to see that each end is in acceptable position, and quickly loosen the clamps to reposition the end pieces if there has been any squirming. Because using only one bar clamp could allow the boxes to jump out of the clamping arrangement, set the boxes down on the floor or table top with the clamp up. Leave the clamp in place for several hours to make sure the glue has an opportunity to set firmly.

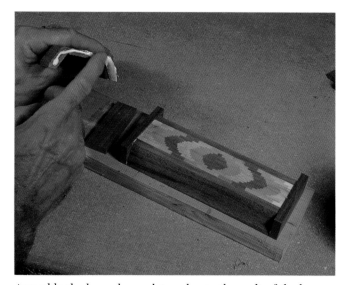

Assemble the boxes by applying glue to the ends of the box bodies and then placing the end pieces in position. Use a flat scrap board to build a row of the tops and bottoms together, and then use a bar clamp and end blocks to pull the joints tight.

FINAL SHAPING AND SANDING

STEP 1
Trim the End Pieces
Cut the corners off the end pieces with the table saw, with the blade still tilted at the same angle as for defining the outside shape. Move the fence over just a little to allow for some of the end pieces to be sanded off.

STEP 2
Rough Sand the Sides
Use the stationary belt sander to sand the box ends even with the tops and bottoms. Sand the tops, bottoms, angles, sides and the flat areas where the tops and bottoms will come together, starting out with 100-grit and moving to 150-grit.

Cut the corners off the end pieces with the table saw, with the blade still tilted at the same angle as for defining the outside shape.

Use a belt sander to sand the box ends even with the tops and bottoms.

Using the router table, cut the spaces for the hinges to fit.

INSTALLING THE HINGES

STEP 1
Cut the Hinge Mortises
Once the rough sanding is complete, and prior to orbital sanding, cut the mortises for the 1"-wide hinges to fit. Do this on the router table by setting up a stop block on the table to control the movement of the box over the 1" router bit. Set the height of the router bit at just under half the thickness of the hinge. After cutting one mortise in the top and bottom, relocate the stop block to route the matching mortises.

STEP 2
Predrill Screw Holes for the Hinges
Use a jig to make sure the holes for the hinges are placed properly, and predrill for the hinges with a $\frac{1}{16}$" drill bit. Use a bit of beeswax on the threads of the screws to lubricate them so they don't break off in the hole. Before the final sanding, sand the ends and front edge of the assembled box on the belt sander to make sure they are in perfect alignment. Then do the finish sanding with a random orbit sander, going from 180-grit to 240-grit, and finishing with 320.

FINISHING

I originally used Deft semi-gloss Clear Wood Finish to finish these boxes, polishing them smooth with 0000 steel wool between the two coats, and again when the finish was dry to soften the gloss enough to hide any irregularities in the brushed-on surface. Now I use Deft Danish Oil, which I prefer because it is a wipe-on, wipe-off finish that does not smell as bad as the lacquer-based Deft. I am careful to keep the shop well ventilated during my finishing operations, and I spread the used rags out outdoors to fully dry before disposing of them.

CHAPTER 2

The Art of Inlay

nlay is perceived to be a more advanced woodworking technique requiring a great deal of patience and skill and, for this reason, many woodworkers are reluctant to try it. It is easy to create your own inlays and use them to enhance your woodworking projects. Making inlay, for me, is a form of workshop play; an opportunity to experiment and see what I can come up with. The woods themselves, the colors, the patterns of grain, their various levels of reflectivity of light and their smells as they pass through the saw, are a source of enjoyment for me. For some woodworkers, doing inlay work is a way they can demonstrate their woodworking expertise. Personally, I like to use my craftsmanship to give voice to the natural characteristics of the wood, and use the inlay techniques to focus attention on the wood's beauty rather than on my skill as a craftsman.

MAKING CHECKERBOARD INLAY

STEP 1
Prepare the Stock
Start by cutting ½″ × 1¼″ blocks of crotch walnut and fiddleback maple from ¾″ × 1¼″ stock. Use the sliding cutoff table on the table saw, and a stop block to maintain uniformity.

STEP 2
Arrange and Glue the First Pattern
After the pieces are cut, arrange them in an alternating pattern—walnut, maple, walnut—forming a long string of patterned blocks. After you have organized the pattern, apply glue to all surfaces that contact other surfaces and then use a bar clamp to pull them tight, as shown in making the inlay for the simple inlaid box in the previous chapter. To keep them flat and straight, glue them up on a flat board, removing them from the board when the clamp is tight. Sight down the glued-up stock to ensure that the row of blocks is still straight, and shim the row out away from the bar or clamp it toward the bar, if necessary.

STEP 3
Rip ½″ Strips From the Inlay Pattern
After the glue has had plenty of time to set up, joint two edges flat and square on the jointer, set up the table saw with a thin-kerf crosscut blade and rip the strip into two ½″-wide strips. These two strips will be glued back together, offset to form the ½″ squares.

STEP 4
Glue-Up the New Pattern
Use two ⅛″-thick walnut strips as border stock, and spread glue on each surface to be glued. Use long strips of wood to cushion and distribute the pressure from the bar clamps, and use about six clamps to glue a 30″ section.

STEP 5
Cut the Inlay
After this block has been glued for several hours, unclamp it and joint one face on the jointer. Then set up the table saw with a thin-kerf ripping blade and saw the inlay block into thin strips (³⁄₃₂″ to ⅛″ thick). Use a zero-clearance insert in the table saw to reduce risk of the inlay coming apart or jumping around while ripping the strips. The finished inlay is 1¼″ wide, and you get about five strips from the gluing-and-cutting procedure.

Use the cutoff box on the table saw and a stop block to make sure all the pieces are the same size. The cutoff box is a simple jig that rides in the grooves in the table saw top allowing accurate cutting of parts.

After arranging the blocks in the alternating pattern, apply glue to the end grain on both ends before placing pieces back in the arrangement.

MAKING THE TRIANGLE INLAY

Cut Angled Pieces

To make the triangle-pattern inlay, use the cutoff box on the table saw with a fence made of a piece of plywood tacked on the surface of the table with brads. The exact angle used for this is not critical: Turning the stock over between cuts will give each piece the same angle on each side to ensure fitting with neighboring pieces. I used sassafras, pecan and honey locust to cut the triangles for this inlay.

STEP 2

Assemble the Pattern

To assemble this pattern, spread glue on each piece alternating the species of wood in a pecan, honey locust, sassafras, pecan pattern. After spreading glue on the ⅛" walnut border strips, clamp the parts together using bar clamps and hardwood blocks to keep the inlay block straight.

OTHER VARIETIES

The number of patterns that can be made is infinite. By gluing simple strips of wood together and cutting the glued-up block into angled slices, I make another simple but pleasing design. To glue-up a pattern like this requires extra care to keep the parts in alignment, so clamp side blocks in place to keep parts from shifting while the bar clamp pulls the pieces tightly together.

NOW, DESIGN YOUR OWN

I invite you to use these simple processes as your own jumping-off point into this form of workshop play and experimentation. You will come up with many ideas of your own.

Use the cutoff box and angled guide with a stop block to cut uniform triangles for the patterned inlay.

After arranging the pieces in the pattern, spread glue on all sides of each triangle and the walnut border strips. Use bar clamps and hardwood blocking to clamp the parts together, forming a block of inlay that will yield several inlay strips.

With the cutoff box, cut thin slices from a block formed of various hardwoods.

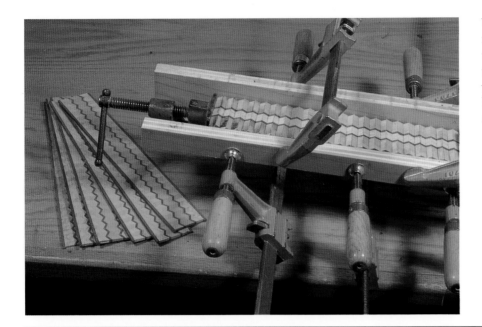

With the slices alternating, glue them back together into a patterned block, which, when resawn on the band saw, will yield several inlay strips.

SLIDING CUTOFF TABLE

The sliding cutoff table is a simple device that I use to accurately cut parts to uniform length. For example, when cutting the front and back of a box, the most important thing is not the exact length in terms of inches, but that both parts be exactly the same length. By using a stop block clamped to the fence of the cutoff table and by pushing the workpiece against the stop block, each piece cut will be exactly the same. This is important whether cutting parts for a single box or twenty, because when working on the small scale that boxes present, even $\frac{1}{64}$" can be noticed in the opening and closing of a lid. I frequently use a cutoff table without the fence when cutting very small and irregularly shaped parts. If you have ever tried to hold something really small safely using a standard miter gauge,

you know the difficulties involved. As shown in some of the projects of the book, I just use small brads to secure fences made of $\frac{1}{4}$" plywood at a variety of angles as needed to make various small parts, and small stop blocks secured with brads to help hold the parts in the exact position needed. In this way, I can set up using very simple and direct methods for making accurately dimensioned small and angled parts. One word of caution: You must remember that the blade, in making a through cut, will appear on the other side of the fence, unguarded. I am very careful to keep my hands and other items, such as already cut parts, out of the line of cut. It's easy to construct a cutoff table with a simple guard at the back side and, using my best judgment, I recommend it.

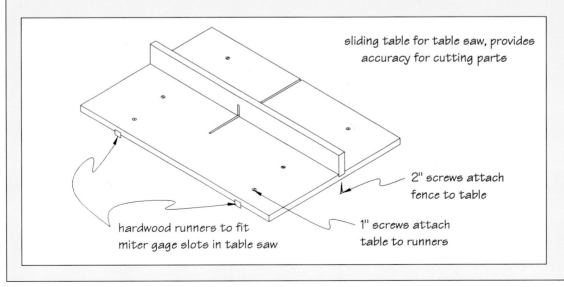

sliding table for table saw, provides accuracy for cutting parts

2" screws attach fence to table

1" screws attach table to runners

hardwood runners to fit miter gage slots in table saw

CHAPTER 3

The Koa Box

This box is made from a piece of koa brought to me by my Hawaiian cousins. Made with a simple band-saw technique, a block of wood is cut apart into components and then glued back together, leaving out the parts that had formed the interior space. This is a very popular technique and simple enough for a beginner to have success with, building his or her skills in the use of the band saw or scroll saw. Many woodworkers have used these basic techniques to develop creative and artistic work. Making a box like this is fun, as much like play as wood "working." I decided to make two, cutting them apart after defining the interior compartments.

SHAPING THE BOX

STEP 1

Cutting Away the Top and Bottom

Begin this box by cutting away the bottom and top from the block of koa using the band saw. Carefully check the tracking of the band saw blade before you start so that you are able to cut uniform ¼"-thick slices from the top and bottom. Next, resurface all the pieces to remove the band saw marks and to provide a good gluing surface when the pieces go back together.

STEP 2

Cut Out the Interior

Draw the desired interior shape onto the block using found objects to define the space from the center of the original block. I used a can and a washer for this one. Scroll saw carefully into one corner from the outside and then saw around the perimeter, forming the inside of the box. A band saw can also be used for this.

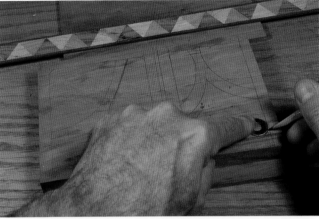

Use found objects to lay out the design. Here I use a washer to give shape to a corner.

On the scroll saw, follow the cut line to define the interior of the box.

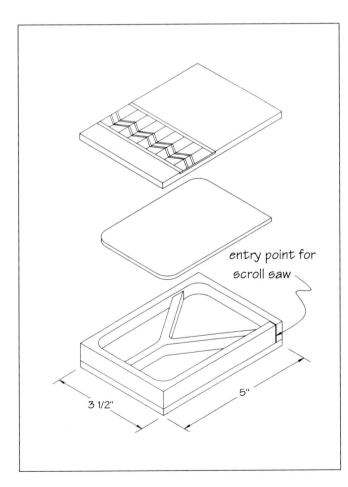

entry point for scroll saw

3 1/2"

5"

MATERIALS LIST		
Hawaiian koa	1 pc.	1 b.f. × 1⅛"
Strips of pecan, sassafras and honey locust		¾" × 1"
Strips of walnut		⅛" × ¾" (for inlay)

TOOLS LIST	
Scroll saw	Band saw
Router	Table saw
Router table	Belt sander
Orbital sander	

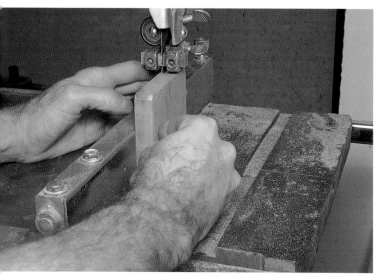
Cut away a thin slice of the waste pieces to use as the parts of the lids that locate their positions on the boxes.

Return to your found objects to mark the center waste pieces for cutting out the dividers.

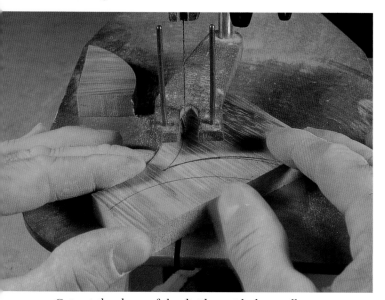
Cut out the shape of the dividers with the scroll saw.

Remove the Lid Keeper and Interior Dividers

Set up the ripping fence on the band saw, setting the fence about ³⁄₁₆″ from the blade so that you can surface the lid keeper to about ⅛″ before gluing it to the lid. Cut the divider for the inside of the box from the remaining piece. Use the found objects again to mark out the interior dividers and cut out the divider parts with the scroll saw. Hand sand the inside of the box and the divider, using a small rasp to clean up some of the tight spots. Sandpaper can be used with a flat stick for the convex areas, and wrapped on a dowel for some of the concave parts of the divider. Because the box will be lined with flocking, don't worry about achieving a perfect finish. The flocking will cover the sanding marks.

ASSEMBLING THE BOX

STEP 1
Mark and Glue the Lid Keepers

Trace out the position of the lid keepers with a pencil, marking their location for gluing to the inside of the lid. Then spread glue on the parts and clamp them in the position indicated by the pencil lines. Spread glue on the box body where it intersects the bottom, and use a business card to work a little glue into the saw kerf left when the inside piece was cut away. Fill the saw kerf with a thin sliver of wood and use a bar clamp to squeeze this joint closed, and then clamp the bottom in place with several C-clamps. Since you will use a flocked lining, don't worry too much if a little glue squeezes out; it can easily be cleaned away with a small chisel when it is slightly dry but still rubbery.

MAKING THE INLAY

Inlay this box after it is fully assembled. Making the inlay used in this box is described in detail in chapter two.

FLOCKING THE INTERIOR

I use Donjer Flocking (see Sources) to line the inside of the box. To use this product, brush on the colored adhesive and then either spray on the rayon flocking material with the flocking sprayer or simply put a few tablespoons of flocking material in the box, close the lid and shake.

Spread glue on the inside lid parts and clamp them to the lid stock. You can see how the lid "keeper" locks the lid in place.

Use a pencil to trace the inside shape of the box on the lid to accurately position the inside parts of the lid.

Spread glue on the midsections of the box and then clamp them to the box bottom.

OUR GLOBAL FOREST

As I began my woodworking career, my community of Eureka Springs, Arkansas, was undergoing rapid growth, and I watched as many acres of hardwood and pine forests were bulldozed for new gas stations and motels, and thousands of acres more in the surrounding area were bulldozed to create pastures for livestock. In many cases the trees were not harvested, but simply pushed into ravines or into a pile and burned. During this time as well, it was U.S. Forest Service policy in Arkansas to spray large tracts of hardwoods with defoliants to kill them and allow the faster-growing pines to take over. It became obvious to me that the woods which brought such excitement and wonder to my life were seen as having little value in our culture. It became my hope that by using our hardwoods in a way that informed others of their value, I might become part of a dialogue leading to their being cherished in our society. We live in a single global forest. The wood thrush that sings in the forest around my home in the summer has a winter life in tropical forests far beyond our national boundary. A woodworker friend shares the following story. He is a wood carver who, despite years of using exotic tropical woods in his work and having a strong fascination with their beauty, had become very concerned about the environmental issues surrounding their use. One day he and his wife were outside his workshop discussing his interest in changing his work to use domestic wood exclusively. She believed that the sale of his work would suffer. He was hoping to find the courage to make the change. And while they talked, a ruby throated hummingbird swooped down and struck him right in the chest. It was an omen that my friend would not ignore. I urge those who work with wood to also work with trees and forests. Whether we choose to use domestic or tropical woods, we have a responsibility to our global forest. When the wood thrush sings in my ten acre wood, I rejoice that somewhere on another continent she still has a home in winter. Some of the ways we can support our global forest are: Plant trees, buy land and protect it from development, join and support organizations like Global Releaf, the World Wildlife Federation and The Nature Conservancy. Use care in cutting, avoid waste, reuse or compost your sawdust. Make beautiful, well-crafted things that future generations will cherish.

CHAPTER 4

The Pen Box

Making the pen box is a very simple exercise in box building and a skill builder. The commercial inlays are easy to use, and while it is my feeling that they do not have as much character or personal interest as those I make in my shop, they can very well enhance the beauty of simple projects. Offsetting the location of the inlay toward the front endge of the lid gives the user an indication of which side to open, and is more visually stimulating than having the inlay centered in the box top. This box can be easily modified to meet a number of uses, but as in the simple inlaid box in chapter one, I would hesitate to make it very large because of the stresses involved in the expansion and contraction of wood.

MAKING THE PEN BOX

STEP 1
Form the Box Interior

Forming the interior shape of the box is done on the table saw. Set the height of the cut to leave about 3/16″ of material at the bottom of the box, and cut the entire length at the same time. Since you want the top of the box to be smaller in proportion than the bottom, plane down the top, removing material from the open side of the box.

STEP 2
Cut the Box to Length

Cut the box parts using the cutoff box on the table saw.

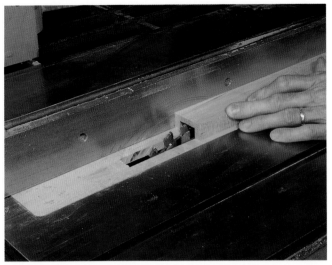

MATERIALS LIST		
Cherry		$^{13}/_{16}''\times3^1/_2''\times24''^1$
Top and bottom	2 pcs.	$2^3/_4''\times2''\times6''$
Ends	2 pcs.	$2^3/_4''\times1^3/_4''\times1^1/_4''$
5mm barrel hinges	4 pcs.	
Commercial inlay		

[1]This yields enough stock for two boxes.

TOOLS LIST	
Table saw	$^1/_{16}''$ roundover bit
Chamfering bit	5mm brad-point bit
Drill press	Router table with straight-cut
Bar clamp	bits

Cut the inside shape of the pen box with a dado blade, cutting the top and bottom of the cherry box in a single operation and moving the fence to widen the cut.

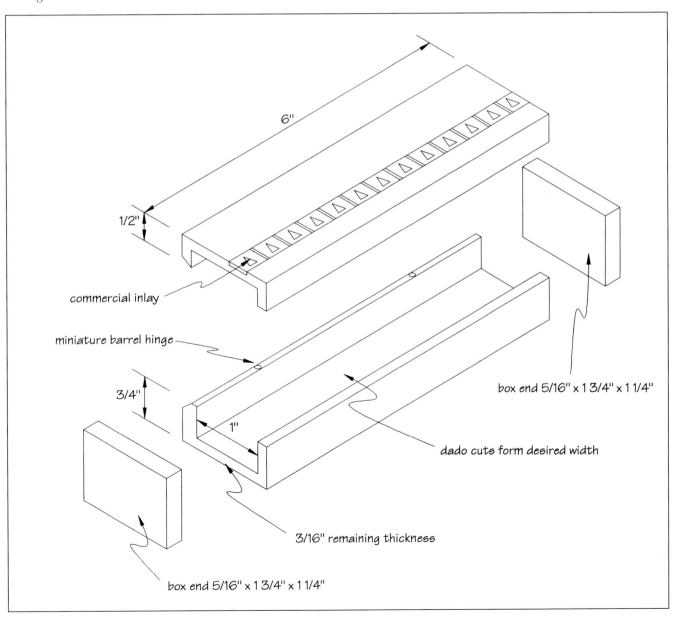

commercial inlay

miniature barrel hinge

6"

1/2"

3/4"

1"

box end 5/16" x 1 3/4" x 1 1/4"

dado cuts form desired width

3/16" remaining thickness

box end 5/16" x 1 3/4" x 1 1/4"

STEP 3
Drill Holes for the Barrel Hinges

As in making the spalted maple box in chapter eight, drill to fit the miniature barrel hinges after carefully drilling a test piece and checking the depth with a dial caliper. To set up for drilling perfectly matched holes, left and right, first drill the holes on one side of all the parts, using a stop block clamped onto the fence on the drill press. Then drill through a piece of scrap wood and turn that over, using it to set the stop on the fence to position the other holes. This gives left and right holes that match perfectly. To compensate for the differing thickness of the top and bottom, use a shim piece rather than change the depth of the drilling to adjust the height. You can see this operation in detail in chapter twelve.

STEP 4
Inlay the Top

To inlay the top, select a straight-cut router bit equal to the width of the inlay strip, raise the cutter height to just barely less than the thickness of the strip and set the fence to position the strip off-center to indicate which side opens. Then route the channel for the inlay strip. The commercial inlay is sized to slip right in place. Spread a little glue in the channel, and use a strip of wood cut just a little narrower than the inlay strip as a block to distribute clamping pressure.

STEP 5
Chamfer the Edges

Route a 45° chamfer on the back edges on the box tops and bottoms to clear for the hinges.

STEP 6
Make the Ends

Resaw a bit of cherry to make the ends. It is far safer to resaw a length of 15″ or 16″ using the table saw so the piece can be grabbed safely from the other side of the blade. Cut the ends for these boxes on the band saw, and plane them to 5⁄16″ thick.

STEP 7
Glue the Ends in Place

Lightly sand the inside edges before gluing on the ends. Spread glue on the ends of the bottom pieces and then clamp the end pieces in place with a bar clamp, using clamping blocks to avoid marring the wood.

STEP 8
Trim the Lid to Fit

After the glue has dried, trim the lid a very slight amount shorter—a hair from each end—to give side clearance for opening the box.

With a straight-cut router bit set to just under the thickness of the commercial inlay strip, route the channel for the inlay.

STEP 9
Insert the Hinges

Insert the hinges with just a bit of glue in the holes, and then sand the top, sides and ends flush on the 6″ × 48″ belt sander. Start out with a coarse grit to bring the surfaces even, moving to a finer grit before sanding the inlay flush with the lid. Before orbital sanding, use the chamfering bit in the router table to lightly chamfer the ends of the boxes, sand with the inverted orbital sander, and finish with three coats of Danish oil.

Use a 45° chamfering bit in the router to provide clearance to operate the hinges.

ZERO-CLEARANCE INSERT

The zero-clearance insert for the table saw is an essential item for ripping thin stock for making inlay. I've been using one for about twenty years, without knowing what to call it, but then saw a magazine article mentioning it. The purpose of the zero-clearance insert is to give better support to thin stock which might slip down into a standard insert, creating a dangerous situation for the woodworker. It also helps in preventing tear-out on the underside of the board. You will find in operating a table saw, that the mass of the workpiece is inversely related to smoothness of the cutting operation. When you cut a piece of wood thinner and thinner through a number of ripping operations, the piece will begin to chatter and feel less certain to the operator. It is when the workpiece reaches the thinner stages, and the stock is least well supported by the saw table that the zero-clearance insert becomes most necessary. I make my zero-clearance inserts of maple, and I usually make several blanks at a time, since these are disposable items.

I plane maple stock down to the thickness of the recessed area of the table saw top, and then clamp a guide template on it and route it with a template-following router bit, as used in shaping the doors on

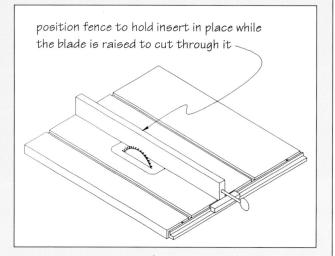

position fence to hold insert in place while the blade is raised to cut through it

the Fiddleback maple jewelry chest, chapter sixteen. With the insert blank in place, I turn the saw on and gradually raise the blade as it cuts through the insert. A good safety measure is to cover a portion of the insert, with the fence of the saw table clamped in place on the side of the insert, just away from where the blade will raise through. This will enable you to give your full attention to the matter of slowly raising the blade.

CHAPTER 5

The Stamp Box

A few simple techniques can be used to create a variety of boxes, and can be a fun way to exercise one's creativity while making something useful. These small boxes use the drill press to form the inside of the box and a custom jig (of my own invention) on the router table to form the lid. This technique can be used on small pieces of wood as misshapen as walnut burl, and can be used in various partnerships with some of the inlay techniques presented in this book. This technique can inspire boxes in various shapes, sizes and uses. While most of these boxes could be done on the lathe as well, this technique provides tight-fitting lids with very little effort.

MATERIALS LIST		
Walnut (or other wood)		1⅜″ × 1⁵⁄₁₆″ × 3″
Other wood for inlay	2 pcs.	3″ long

TOOLS LIST	
Table saw	Jointer
Planer	Router table with custom fence
¾″ or 1″ straight-cut router bit	Drill press with 1″ diameter Forstner or carbide bit

MAKING THE BOX

STEP 1
Install the Inlay

To make an inlaid stamp box, start by doing the inlay on a block of wood, but leave a space between the parts of the inlay to allow for the lid to be cut away and for the lip to be formed.

STEP 2
Make a Pivot Fence Jig

While waiting for the glue to dry, make a pivot fence for the router table, as shown in the drawing below. Use a nail with the head removed as a pivot pin that the lid can turn on, and leave one end of the router table's fence loose so it can pivot on the opposite end. Then locate the center of the lid and drill into it with another nail with the head removed (the same size as the one used as a pivot pin in the router jig).

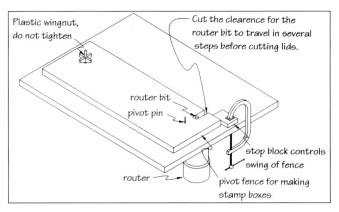

Plastic wingnut, do not tighten

Cut the clearence for the router bit to travel in several steps before cutting lids.

router bit

pivot pin

stop block controls swing of fence

router

pivot fence for making stamp boxes

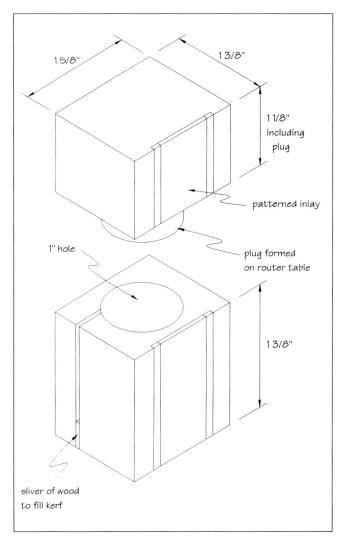

15/8"

13/8"

1 1/8" including plug

patterned inlay

plug formed on router table

1" hole

13/8"

sliver of wood to fill kerf

Start by inlaying the stock for the boxes, leaving spaces in the inlay where the lid will be cut away and the lip will be formed.

After cutting the inlaid block into sections, drill a small hole in the tops to fit the pivot pin on the router table fence.

STEP 3
Make a Test Cut

To set up the jig for routing the lips on the lids, start by drilling a test hole in a scrap piece so you can accurately adjust the travel of the pivot fence and control the diameter of the finished lid. Then cut a test lid from a scrap piece, and adjust the fence stop to either tighten or loosen the fit of the test lid in the test hole.

STEP 4
Cut the Lid

When you are satisfied with the fit, route the lips on the box tops. Either before or after forming the lips, insert a shortened nail into the pivot hole on the lid and use it to locate the position for the next step: drilling the hole in the base. Squeezing the parts together along a straight-edge (such as the back edge of the router fence) will help to align them accuarately.

The pivoting fence on the router table allows you to take very small cuts into the block, which is held in place by the pin. Rather than turn the block on the pivot pin, pivot the entire fence in toward the stop block and then back off, turn the block slightly on the pin and pivot the fence again, repeating this process until most of the waste is removed. Then you can safely twist the block on the pivot pin, accurately sizing it to fit the hole in the base. Be careful not to take too large a cut, as the router bit can grab and twist the workpiece out of control.

A SIMPLE ROUTER TABLE

I have two router tables in my shop that I use regularly. Both are simple, flat boards with router bases secured underneath by machine screws; both have pivoting fences. The reasons for the pivoting fence arrangement are, first, it is so simple to use—I position it by moving a single "C" clamp, and can set it up by clamping it to any of the workbenches in my shop; second, it is accurate for fitting parts requiring very close tolerances.

Imagine that the distance between the cutter and fence is controlled by moving the outboard end of the fence. If the router is placed at half the distance from the pivot point to the outside edge of the table, then a movement of the fence of $\frac{1}{64}''$ would amount to a movement of the fence of $\frac{1}{128}''$ or half the distance when measuring from the router bit to the fence. You can see that it is possible to get very close tolerances easily and quickly. Please remember that, as I discuss measurements, my real interest is in fit and not a numerical scale. I usually do not concern myself with measuring sixty-fourths or one hundred twenty-eighths, but with how a part actually fits.

Plastic wingnut

3/4" plywood table

plastic insert

machine screws

hardwood fence
secured with clamp

router

edge shaped to
arc of fence pivot

Insert a short, sharpened pin in the top of the box and, squeezing it to the base, mark the location of the hole to be drilled.

Use a 1″ drill to hollow the insides to fit a standard roll of stamps, or 1⅛″ for the self-adhesive roll stamps.

FORMING THE INTERIOR OF THE BOX

STEP 1
Drill the Interior

The interior of the box is formed by drilling the piece of inlaid hardwood. Since you already have the center of the box laid out, simply drill with a 1″ Forstner bit to a depth of 1″ plus the amount necessary for the lip on the box lid to fit.

STEP 2
Make the Slot for the Stamps

To form the slot for stamps to be pulled from the box, use the band saw, cutting in only until the blade enters the hollow left by the drill. Then use a small sliver of matching hardwood to fill the cut at the bottom, leaving space for the stamps to emerge.

FINISHING THE BOX

Use a ⅛″ roundover bit to shape the edges of the stamp box and sand it on the inverted orbital sander as shown in chapter eight. Apply three coats of Danish oil to finish the box.

Use the band saw to cut into the side of the box where the stamps will come out.

Glue a sliver of hardwood into the saw kerf, leaving only the opening necessary for the stamps to emerge.

CHAPTER 6

The Triangle Box

This is a very simple box, impractical, artistic and easy to make. It is made of black walnut and inlaid with spalted maple, or could be inlaid attractively with the triangle pattern from the koa box (chapter three). As it is difficult to glue end grain without mechanical fasteners—dovetails, splines, finger joints, screws or nails—the triangle box is made with the grain running vertically, giving good opportunity for successful gluing without making the project very complicated.

MAKING THE TRIANGLE BOX

STEP 1
Prepare the Stock
Start by resawing 4/4 walnut stock right down the middle on the band saw, and then plane the material to about ¼" thick. Joint one edge of the stock on the jointer before ripping it to the desired width on the table saw. Next cut three equal lengths of stock.

STEP 2
Make the Angled Inlay Guide

Make a guide for routing the angled channel for the diagonal inlay to fit. Take a piece of ¼" plywood scrap and, laying the piece of wood that you intend to inlay on top of it at the angle you want, trace around the wood with a pencil. Then use the band saw to cut the shape out of the scrap wood, so that the scrap wood becomes a guide for carrying the workpiece along the router table fence to route the inlay channel.

STEP 3
Cut the Inlay Channel

After completing the guide piece, set up the router so that the height of the 1" straight-cut bit is just a bit lower than the thickness of the inlay, which you've cut using the method described in chapter seven. Adjust the fence to position the cutter so that it will cut the channel in the workpiece, using the guide piece you've made. Route the first piece with the guide piece moving along the fence and the workpiece held firmly by hand pressure on the guide. To reverse the pattern for the adjoining workpiece, turn the guide end over end and route the second piece. The two front pieces of the box will be mirror images of each other. If you want to widen the channel to accommodate wider inlay, move the fence away from the cutter and perform the two operations again.

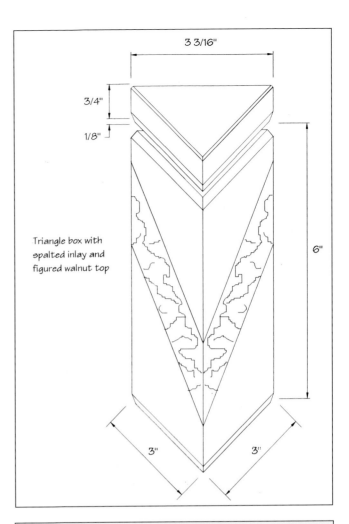

Triangle box with spalted inlay and figured walnut top

Make an angled inlay guide by taking a piece of ¼" plywood scrap and, laying the piece of wood that you plan to inlay on top of it at the angle intended, trace around the wood with a pencil. Cut away the waste with the band saw.

MATERIALS LIST

Plywood or particle board		¼" (for making a jig)
Baltic birch plywood		⅛" (for the bottom)
Walnut		¾" × 3¼" × 13"
Spalted maple for inlay		
Bottom	1 pc.	⅛" × 2⁹⁄₁₆" (each side)
Spalted inlay	2 pcs.	1½" × 6¼" (size to fit)
Sides	2 pcs.	3¼" × 3" × 6"
Top	1 pc.	⅞" × 3³⁄₁₆" (each side)

TOOLS LIST

Band saw	The following cutters:
Jointer	1" straight-cut bit
Router table	¹⁄₁₆"-radius roundover bit
Planer	chamfering bit
Table saw	

The scrap wood becomes a guide for carrying the workpiece along the fence to route the channel for the inlay. Route one side with the guide piece face down; turn the guide piece over to route the other piece.

Because the two sides mirror each other, glue them up at the same time, clamping them together with blocking between.

STEP 4
Install the Inlay

Next, size the inlay pieces to fit (as described in making the simple inlaid box in chapter one). Cut the angled pieces oversized in length using the miter guide on the table saw, select the pattern carefully so that the two angled sides appear related in color and pattern, and then glue the pieces in place. Put a thin strip of wood between the two sides and backing pieces to prevent marring from the C-clamps, making a sandwich with the inlay pieces and backing in the middle.

MAKING THE ANGLED SIDES

STEP 1
Trim the Inlay

After the glue holding the inlay in place has dried, trim the spalted wood even with the walnut using a flush-laminate trimming bit in the router. Place the inlaid parts facedown on the router table and use the guide bearing on the bit to follow the walnut, leaving the spalted wood flush with the walnut edge.

STEP 2
Cut the Angled Sides

To cut the pieces so that their angles intersect requires a simple jig, since table saws do not tilt to cut a 30° angle

The flush trim router bit makes quick work of trimming the inlay.

This jig enables you to cut the sides at 30°. This is not possible using the setting on your table saw.

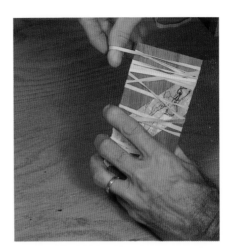

Use large rubber bands to hold the pieces tightly in alignment as the glue dries.

with the workpiece flat on the table. I made a jig that follows the miter slot in the table saw to hold the workpiece vertical as it slides through the saw. Set the angle of the saw at 60°, and clamp the workpiece in place on the jig so that one edge is flush with the surface of the table saw. Cut one edge and then the other of each of the three pieces that form the sides of the box. Of course, it is a good idea to cut test pieces to check the exact intersection of the angles rather than ruin nicely inlaid parts.

STEP 3
Cut the Groove for the Bottom
After the angles have been cut, set up the crosscut table on the table saw, adjust the blade height to only about 1/8", and set a stop block to position a 1/8" dado cut, which will hold the bottom panel. Make this cut about 1/4" from the bottom edges of the parts.

STEP 4
Make the Bottom
For the bottom use 1/8" Baltic birch plywood, which is cut to shape on the band saw. Cut it deliberately undersized to allow for the contraction of the box body during the dry seasons. Measure the length of the dado cut across the side parts to determine the dimensions of the bottom, with each side of the triangle being a bit less than the length of the dado cut.

ASSEMBLING THE BOX

STEP 1
Round the Edges
Use a 1/16" roundover bit in the router to put a smooth edge on the inside edges of the body of the box; lightly hand sand these edges with 240-grit sandpaper.

STEP 2
Apply Glue and Assemble
Spread glue on each edge, position the bottom in place and hold the three pieces together. Use rubber bands as clamps to apply pressure to the joints, and leave them in place as the glue dries.

MAKING THE TOP

STEP 1
Transfer the Angle to the Top
Make the top out of crotch-figured black walnut. Cut and plane a piece to about 7/8" thick. Use a sliding T-bevel to transfer the 60° angle from the assembled box to the wood for the top, marking out the size just a bit larger than the size of the box, and then cut out the top.

STEP 2
Cut the Lip for the Lid
After the top is cut to shape, sand away the saw marks using the belt sander. Set up the router table with the straight-cut bit to cut the lip where the lift-off lid fits into the box body.

SANDING AND FINISHING

Sand the outside surfaces of the box on the belt sander, bringing the inlay flush with the walnut sides and moving from 100-grit to 150-grit. Route the bottom edge, the top edge and the lid with a 45° chamfering bit on the router. Orbital sand through 180-, 240- and 320-grits, and then hand sand the corners of the box to take off the sharp feel. Finish with three coats of Danish oil.

CHAPTER 7

The Bracelet Box

This bracelet box derived from the simple inlaid box, was the presentation box for a Christmas present for my wife, Jean, in 1995. The gift, a beaded bracelet with warm earth-toned glass beads with a clasp of natural amber, was made by a friend of mine, Eleanor Lux. I decided that the best way to wrap it would be in a walnut box, so I designed this quick presentation box. Jean likes it as much as her beautiful bracelet. Its appearance can be modified through the use of any of the inlay techniques shown in this book; its size can be easily modified to fit the presentation needs of a particular piece of jewelry.

MAKING THE BOX

STEP 1
Cut the Inlay

Cut the inlay from a block of spalted maple using a thin-kerf 50-tooth blade, which gives a very smooth cut. To avoid chattering of the thin stock, use a zero-clearance insert in the opening of the table saw. This securely supports the inlay strips as they are cut. Never cut short pieces of spalted material in this manner, as short pieces are much more dangerous to handle. It is safer to cut them on the band saw and sand the surface that's to be glued.

MATERIALS LIST		
Walnut		
Top and bottom	2 pcs.	¾″ × 1¾″ × 8½″
Ends	2 pcs.	⁵⁄₁₆″ × 1¼″ × 1⅞″
Spalted maple		
Inlay	1 pc.	³⁄₃₂″ × 1⅜″ × 9″

TOOLS LIST	
Stationery belt sander	Standard ⅛″-kerf finish-cut blade
Thin-kerf finish-cut blade	Router table with ¾″ or 1″ straight-cut bit
45° chamfering bit	C-clamps and one bar clamp
Table saw	

The thin-kerf blade gives a smooth surface for gluing, with very little waste.

STEP 2
Make the Top

To make the lift-off lid, cut a piece of walnut the same width as the base, using a pivoting jig mounted to the band saw to cut a smooth curve. The base of the jig is clamped to the table of the band saw, while the upper part pivots

on a 23″ radius. After sawing the lid to shape, sand it on the 6″ × 48″ belt sander. At this point in sanding, you are not aiming for a perfect finish, but rather for a smooth contour for inlaying. The coarse sanding marks will actually be helpful later on in making sure that the inlay is not sanded through.

Use a jig made for the band saw to cut the top to its curved shape. This jig is clamped to the band saw table and pivots on a wide radius, giving a smooth curve for bending the inlay.

Finish shaping the top on the belt sander by rocking the workpiece and checking frequently to make sure you are sanding evenly. The band saw marks help to gauge your progress.

STEP 3
Make the Base

Make this box in much the same way as the simple inlaid box in chapter one. Define the interior space with a series of saw kerfs about ⁹⁄₁₆″ deep, slightly wider than the bracelet. Then make angled cuts at about 15° off perpendicular to widen the opening so that the bracelet does not appear to be in a deep hole, allowing more light to illuminate the beads.

STEP 4
Fitting the Lid

With the blade still set at the 15° angle, but lowered to a height of ⅛″, reset the fence to cut the edges of the top to fit exactly into the opening in the base. With the table saw returned to 90°, and the lid on edge against the fence, cut away the remaining edge.

Use either a dado blade or a series of ⅛″ saw cuts to cut away the inside of the box, and then widen the opening by making a 15° cut on each side.

With the saw still at a 15° angle, lower the blade and adjust the fence to cut the top to fit the opening in the base.

INLAYING THE CURVED TOP

STEP 1
Cut the Channel in the Top
Cutting the channel is done much the same way as inlaying a flat surface on the router, but cut it thinner in order for it to bend more easily to the radius of the top. Raise the cutter to almost the thickness of the inlay you plan to use, and then clamp two pieces of thin wood both before and after the cutter. These form a cradle to control the rocking movement of the top as the inlay channel is cut.

With the lid turned on edge and the saw returned to 90°, cut away the remaining edge so the lid fits into the base.

STEP 2
Size the Inlay
When the channel is cut, size the inlay piece in the same manner as for the simple inlaid box in chapter one.

STEP 3
Install the Inlay
Gluing the inlay piece in place requires a special clamping arrangement. Take the piece of wood that was left over when the top was sawn and cut it on the table saw to about ⅛″ narrower than the finished piece of inlay. Use this piece and a backing piece of ⅛″-thick plywood to provide a flat place for the C-clamps to grip and to evenly distribute clamping pressure. Use a piece of scrap wood on the opposite side to prevent the C-clamps from marring the wood. This arrangement, using three or four C-clamps per box top, will provide plenty of clamping pressure.

Here's the fit you are looking for.

Clamp thin stock on the router table to help cradle the lid as you route the channel for the inlay. Notice the thin piece of wood behind my hand forming the front half of the cradle.

After making one edge true on the jointer, pass the strip between the cutter and fence on the router table to size it to fit in the lid. The safety blocking that would normally cover the bit has been removed to show the process.

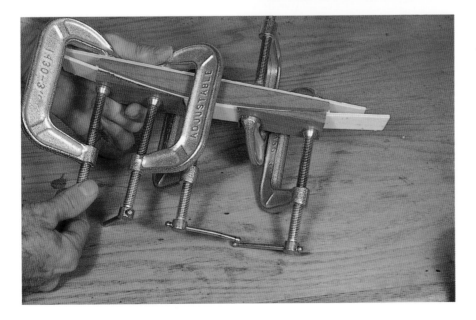

Use the cutoffs from shaping the lid along with a strip of Baltic birch to obtain even clamping pressure.

FINAL ASSEMBLY

STEP 1
Sand the Top

With a sheet of fine sandpaper and working on a very flat surface (the top of the table saw or a smooth workbench), sand the top surfaces of the box body. Then sand the sharp edges, both inside the box and on the outside where they will intersect the lid, slightly round. To match the edge of the box body, lightly sand the edges of the lid with a fine-grit sandpaper to match the sanded edge on the box bottom.

STEP 2
Glue Up the Parts

Using a technique similar to the one used to assemble the simple inlaid box in chapter one, spread glue on the ends of the shaped box body and clamp the end pieces in place with a bar clamp while the glue sets. Unlike the simple inlaid box the ends of this box are cut tall enough to cover the end grain of the lid and give it a resting place when the box is closed.

STEP 3
Trim the Top

Cut the box lid about 1/64" shorter than the inside length of the box. To avoid overcutting and making the lid too loose, clamp a stop block on the cutoff box, cut the box lid to length and check the fit, bumping it over very slightly away from the stop block if it needs to be shorter. The stop block provides a secure frame of reference to keep from cutting away too much.

STEP 4
Final Sanding

When the box top is fitted to the box bottom, hold the pieces together and sand them as a unit on the 6" × 48" belt sander. This quickly shapes the ends to conform to the lid. Because the inlay is thinner than usual, you have to be careful not to sand through; use the coarse sanding markings to ensure that the inlay is not becoming too thin. When the coarse sanding marks are gone, you have sanded enough.

STEP 5
Routing the Edges

Use a 45° chamfering bit in the router to add interest to the edges, routing all edges except the top edge of the ends.

After gluing end pieces on the base, hold the top and bottom together for sanding on the belt sander, using the coarse sanding marks left in forming the box shape as a guide to ensure that you are sanding evenly—but not through—the inlay. When the coarse sanding marks are gone, you have sanded enough.

STEP 6
Finishing

Finish the box by hand-rubbing with three coats of Danish oil.

RELATIONSHIPS

The drawing at right shows a complex set of relationships, within which each of us as a woodworker is unique. We approach our work from a particular focus or set of values. While one of us may be very focused on his tools and the enjoyment he derives from having and using them, another woodworker may be more interested in the materials he uses; still another may be thinking of a small business to supplement his income, or of finding a way of having nice things in the home without having to pay so much for them, and the pride of accomplishment. I am not implying that any particular focus is correct. I believe that we can become better woodworkers by becoming better acquainted with ourselves as woodworkers, knowing our own values enough to establish a more confident direction in our work, and to thereby express more of our own natures in the work we do with wood. We also differ in levels of motivation, self-confidence and experience. Opportunity is my way of describing the encouragement we receive from our environment to do our work. For an amateur, this encouragement may be a spouse or grandchildren with a long list of desires, encouraging our time in the shop and allowing our purchase of the tools and materials necessary for our work. It might take the form of being given the opportunity to work with a particularly rare and beautiful piece of wood, or of finding and falling in love with an ancient band saw, or being given an old plane. For the professional, opportunity could take the form of a market for one's work, providing enough economic return and encouragement to continue. Each woodworker also finds himself or herself in a relationship between tradition and innovation. Tradition is the relationship with other woodworkers, past or present, the way things are done or were done. Innovation is the relationship with the unknown and vast uncharted world of possibilities. It is ironic

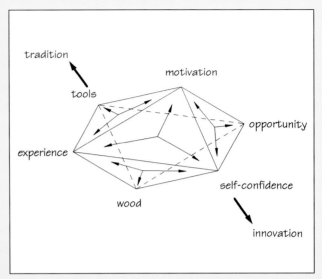

that today, with the widespread use of the router to do every conceivable woodworking operation, it has become innovative to learn what was traditional in woodworking, the use of hand planes and other non-electrical woodworking tools. It is in the balance between tradition and innovation that real creativity takes place. True creativity is not the result of trying to be different, but of allowing one's own unique values within the complex matrix of relationships to be expressed in one's work. It might come from a woodworker's special relationship with a species of wood, or a particular method of work or with a favorite tool. It can center around one's special loving relationship for a wife or girlfriend, or around a personal interest outside the shop—like hunting or fly-fishing. These connections empower our work and give it greater meaning. Woodworking is not something that takes place only in the isolation of our garages and workshops. It is an expression of the complex relationships with the worlds of nature, technology, fellow woodworkers, our friends and family, and even with the growth and discovery of ourselves.

CHAPTER 8

The Walnut Box With Spalted Maple Inlay

This box is one of my current production pieces; I do these in a variety of sizes for sale through galleries nationwide. It is my basic box, which has evolved over a number of years from the simple inlaid box in chapter one. It has a sloping lid—which adds interest to the design, but also serves the very practical purpose of saving wood while allowing appropriate thickness at the rear of the box for the use of miniature barrel hinges. The

spalted maple inlay comes from wood that I have been given by friends, milled myself with a chain saw or had milled by a friend with a portable sawmill, and dried in another friend's greenhouse. In a way, my use of spalted woods is a community effort. Over the years, I've had wood delivered to me by a friend on the parks commission, and the mayor has called to offer me wood from trees fallen along the city streets. Once when a spalted maple had fallen on power lines in front of a home here in Eureka Springs, I was away at a show and friends arranged for a front end loader to lift it and a truck to haul it to my home. It seems sometimes that the wood gathers faster than I can use it, especially when it is cut in ⅛″-thick strips for inlay. My use of spalted woods is an important part of my work: I enjoy revealing this hidden beauty of our forests. I usually mill it about 2½″ thick: This is a reasonable thickness for me to cut on the table saw without too much strain, and it allows some flexibility for use beyond making boxes; for instance, resawing it into panels for small cabinets, drawer facings on chests and other uses. I dry the wood for about a year in the warm and dry conditions of an abandoned, plantless greenhouse before using it. This box is made with mortise-and-tenon joints and a floating panel bottom. It is made to last through many years of seasonal changes in humidity.

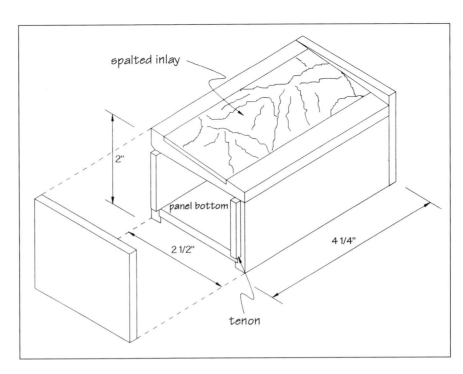

MAKING THE BOX

STEP 1

Preparing the Materials

Cut a 4½″ piece off the end of the 20″ piece of walnut; this piece will be resawn later into the lids for two boxes. Resaw the 20″ piece of walnut on the band saw, using a fence set so that the blade cuts right down the middle. This gives you pieces thick enough to be planed to ⁵⁄₁₆″ thick. From this stock cut fronts, backs, ends and bottoms with the dimensions shown in the materials list at right.

STEP 2

Mortise the End Pieces

Your next step is to mortise the ends for the front, back and bottom to fit. Do this with a ⅛″ router bit mounted in the router table. Adjust the bit to cut to a depth of just over ⅛″, and check your test piece with a dial caliper. (I prefer that the depth be just barely over ⁹⁄₆₄″ to accommodate any variances and allow a space for excess glue when the box is assembled.) Set the fence on the router table so that the outside edge of the cutter is ¹¹⁄₃₂″. When the ⁵⁄₁₆″ sides are in place, this allows ¹⁄₃₂″ to sand level with the sides. Check this measurement with the dial caliper as well, using a test piece. Use stop blocks clamped to the

MATERIALS LIST		
Black walnut		1″ × 3″ × 20″
Spalted maple for inlay		
Miniature barrel hinges	4 pcs.	
Fronts and backs	4 pcs.	1⁵⁄₁₆″ × 3⅞″
Ends	4 pcs.	2⁹⁄₁₆″ × 2⅛″
Bottoms	2 pcs.	2¹⁄₁₆″ × 3¹⁹⁄₃₂″

TOOLS LIST	
Band saw	1″ and ⅛″ straight-cut router bits
Planer	
Router table	⅛″ and ¹⁄₁₆″ roundover bits
6″ × 48″ belt sander	Drill press with 5mm brad-point bit
Jointer	
Table saw	Orbital sander

fence to control the length of the mortises. Set up for a test piece, and when you have set up for the right travel of the workpiece to route the first mortise, cut the mortises in all the ends, positioning each piece between the stops, pressing the workpiece down onto the cutter, moving the piece right-to-left and then left-to-right to clear the mortise of sawdust, finally lifting it off the cutter. Leaving the fence in position, adjust the stop blocks on the fence to route the second mortise on all the ends. Then set up and route the last mortise on all the ends. You will note that

◄ When resawing on the band saw, watch to ensure your blade is tracking well so you end up with two pieces of equal thickness.

Stop blocks on ► the fence ensure the mortises will be the correct length.

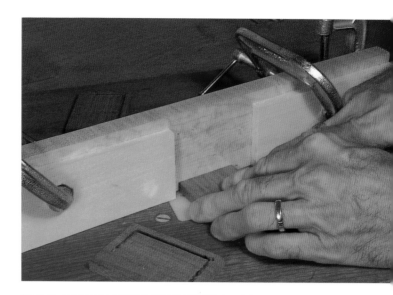

this sequence involves making only one plunge cut on the router table on each end piece, with the subsequent cut starting where the last cut ended.

STEP 3
Cutting the Tenons

Cutting the mortises first allows you to check the tenons and adjust them for the best possible fit. To cut the tenons, use the router table with fence and a 1″ straight-cut router bit. The bit I use has a slight twist in the cutting edges, which gives it a very clean and smooth cut. Set the height of the cutter from the table at exactly ⅛″. Then adjust the fence so that the distance from the inside edge of the cutter and the fence is ⅛″. After these adjustments are made, clamp safety blocks onto the router table to prevent your fingers from having any access to the operating cutter. Cut a test piece standing up along the fence, and move it carefully from right to left. Checking the resulting tenon with the dial caliper tells you whether to raise or lower the cutter by slight increments to obtain tenons exactly ⅛″ long. Check the fit of the tenon in the mortise, and move the fence in or out as necessary to obtain a good fit. What I look for in a good fit is that the tenon will slip into the mortise without difficulty, but is tight enough that, if I hold the mortised end upside down, there is enough friction that the tenoned piece does not fall out without shaking it. When you are satisfied with the tenon cut on the test piece, cut tenons on each end of the front and back pieces.

STEP 4
Cut the Dadoes for the Bottom Panels

Set up the table saw with a ⅛″-kerf blade to cut the dadoes where the bottom panels fit the front and back pieces. Set the blade height so that the center of the cut is ⅛″ deep

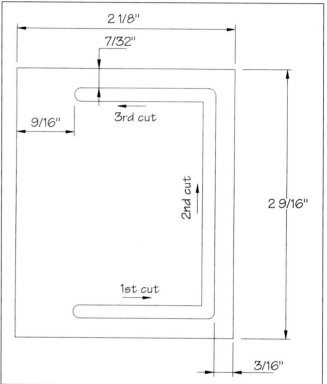

Cut the tenons using the router table with fence and a 1″ straight-cut router bit. The bit I use has a slight twist in the cutting edges, which gives it a very clean and smooth cut. Here, the safety blocking has been removed to show the operation.

A good friction fit tells you your tenon is the right size.

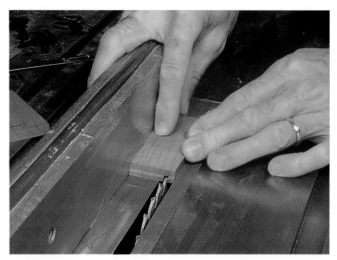

Use the table saw and a blade with a ⅛"-kerf to cut the dadoes ⅛" × ⅛" where the bottom panels fit the front and back pieces.

Using the cutoff box, cut away the nubs on the ends of the front and back pieces.

and the fence is 1" from the blade. This will give the finished box 1" of interior height.

STEP 5
Trim the Tenons

After cutting the dadoes, trim off the little nubs left between the dado and bottom edges, as shown in the drawing at bottom right. To do this, use the cutoff box on the table saw, with the blade raised just enough to cut the nubs off each end and with the stop block adjusted so that the cut is flush with the surface left in tenoning.

STEP 6
Making the Bottom Panels

Use the same router-table setup and settings as used for the tenons to cut the rabbetted edge on the bottom panels where they fit into the end pieces. In order to get a good fit where the panels fit into the dadoes on the fronts and backs, you usually will have to adjust the fence in or out. Notice that in cutting the ends of the panels and the tenons on the fronts and backs, the router setup calls for climb-feeding the stock into the cutter. This involves feeding the wood into the bit in the same direction the bit is turning. This gives a very clean cut when removing end grain. A conventional feed, against the rotation of the bit, can cause unwanted tear-out. This operation requires a very firm hold on the workpiece. Safety blocking must be securely in place to prevent fingers from being pulled into the cutter. If you have not tried a cut like this before, practice with scraps until you feel comfortable with it. The danger is greatly increased when cutting very hard woods, like the tight grain that forms around knots. Climb-feeding is more likely to grab the wood and pull it into the cutter when cutting the rabbets on the sides of the panels, since the

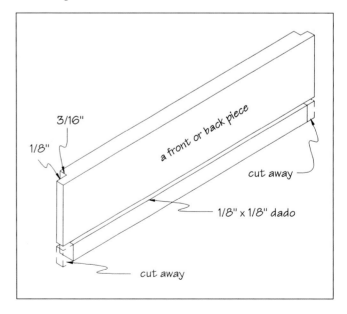

3/16"

1/8"

a front or back piece

cut away

1/8" x 1/8" dado

cut away

long grain does not shear away as easily as the end grain. This operation requires a very firm hand and very close attention. *Never* do this without without safety blocking. Blocking will help prevent fingers from coming in contact with the router bit.

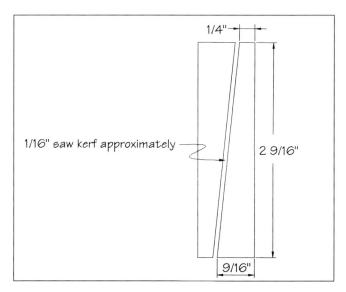

STEP 7
Making the Lids

Plane the material for the tops to ⅞", joint it and rip it to just over 2⁹⁄₁₆" wide, and then joint the ripsawn edge smooth. This gives you enough good stock to band saw the piece into two tops. Rather than set the saw to a particular angle, mark the angle on the end of the workpiece with a line measured as in the drawing at top right. Then adjust the band saw table to the angle marked on the end of the workpiece. Test that the angle and the fence are set just right by cutting slightly into one end and then turning the piece over to see that the band saw blade slips perfectly into the cut. Then cut the piece into material for two box tops.

STEP 8
Inlaying the Top

Select the inlay for the tops of the boxes and cut it to just over the length of the lid. Then route a channel in the tops, following the sequence described for making the simple inlaid box (chapter one). In the finished box, the spalted inlay will be surrounded equally on all sides by a walnut frame. For the 2½" top, with the frame to the right and left being formed by the end pieces (which are ⁵⁄₁₆" thick), the channel inlay will be routed to a width of 1⅞". Start by setting the height of the router bit to nearly the thickness of the inlay above the table, and set the fence so that the 1" straight-cut bit will cut a channel right down the middle of the top. Cut the channel on the band-sawn face. In successive cuts, widen the channel equally by moving the fence further away from the cutter and turning the workpiece end over end. When the cut nears the right width for the inlay piece, make a final thin cut with the workpiece fed into the router in the opposite direction and the fence opening narrowed. This cut will ensure that the channel is uniform throughout its length, since both sides of the channel will be indexed from the same side.

STEP 9
Install the Inlay

When the channel is finished, trim the inlay strip to fit using the router table and the techniques described for making the simple inlaid box (chapter one). Then glue the strips in place. Because the tops are cut at an angle, ar-

Use the router table and a 1″ straight-cut router bit to cut the channel for the spalted inlay. Use the piece of inlay to help set up the height of cut, leaving the bit cutting less than the full thickness of the inlay.

After cutting the channel to the planned width, size the inlay to fit the channel, raising the bit higher than the thickness of the inlay and adjusting the fence so that the opening equals the width of the channel in the lid. Use safety blocking for this operation.

range them face to face, the way they were cut apart at the band saw, with a piece of scrap plywood between them and on the outside to obtain even pressure from the clamps and to prevent the clamps from marring what will be the inside of the lids.

STEP 10

Fitting the Lids

After the tops have been clamped long enough for the glue to set, put one of the boxes together without glue and trim the tops to the length of the inside space between the ends. I like the lids to be about ¼⁴″ shorter than the opening. At this level of tolerance, I can just barely feel movement when I move the lid side to side in the assembled box. Use the cutoff box to accurately make this trim cut.

STEP 11

Fitting the Hinges

Drill the holes for the press-in-place barrel hinges with a 5mm brad-point drill bit in the drill press. Because the backs and lids are different heights and lengths, you have to change the depth of the drilling and the position of the stop blocks to drill these parts. The setting of the fence remains constant. After drilling the holes, chamfer the back edges of the back and lid to clear for the operation of the lid.

Whenever I set up to use any new type of hardware, I play with it a bit to find out what its needs are and how to design and cut for its use. It can be very helpful to do a sample setup with the hinges and sample wooden parts.

STEP 12

Sand the Inside Surfaces

Before final assembly, sand the inside surfaces and ends of the tops. It is easier to do this now than to wait until the box is assembled. Also, route the outside top edge of the front pieces with a ¼⁶″ roundover bit. This creates an obvious place for fingertips to open the finished box.

STEP 13

Final Assembly

Use a small squeeze bottle to apply glue to the insides of the mortises and the end pieces, then slip the fronts, backs and bottom panels in place. If you have obtained a good fit in cutting the tenons, the boxes will go together easily and not need clamping. If the fit is just a little bit loose, rubber bands or tape will do the trick. Before the glue has set up, it is good to check the bottom panels to ensure that the spacing is uniform and to make necessary corrections. This is also the time to press the hinges in place and to attach the lids. Slip the hinges into the holes on the lids with just a drop of woodworker's glue. Then push them partially in place, line them up with the holes on the back sides of the boxes and press them firmly into place until the hinges have seated. Installing the lids now allows you

Glue two boxes at once to make clamping easier; use a spacer between the boxes to keep the lids from gluing to each other and to distribute pressure evenly on the inlay. Additional blocking protects the undersides of the lids from the clamps.

Set up stop blocks on the drill press for controlling the positions of the holes.

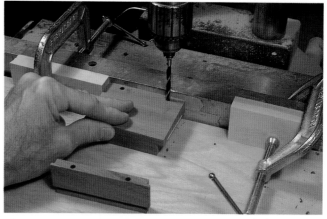

The position of the stop blocks must be changed for the lids, moving the blocks in ⅛″ on each side, because the lids are cut shorter than the tenoned fronts and backs.

Be careful to use just enough glue to do the job without excess squeeze out.

Put just a drop of woodworker's glue into each of the hinge holes, slip the hinges into the holes on the lids, pushing them partially in place, align the lid with the base of the box and squeeze it into position. This is a good time to test the opening and closing of the lid, as this will let you know if the box is assembled square.

to make sure, while you still have time to adjust the fit, the boxes are square in relation to the lids and that they open and close smoothly. If the lid rubs when opening and closing the box, squeeze it corner to corner just a bit to square the box to the lid.

STEP 14
Trim the Ends
After the glue has dried, trim the excess wood from the ends. Use the band saw, with the table tilted so that the blade travels parallel to the face of the box and the fence set up to allow the completed box to pass between the fence and blade with just a small cleanup allowance.

STEP 15
Sanding
Sand the box on the 6″ × 48″ belt sander, starting with 80-grit to sand the inlay, ends and top flush. Use the band saw markings and their gradual disappearance as your guide to even sanding; this way, you avoid sanding through the layer of inlay. Then change belts to 100- or 120-grit and sand all surfaces of the box smooth. Finish the belt sanding with 150-grit.

STEP 16
Routing the Box Edges
Before the final sanding, use the router with the 1/16″ roundover bit installed to round the front inside edge of the lid to match the contour of the front piece. Then mount a 1/8″ roundover bit and route all the edges of the box except the top front edge of the lid.

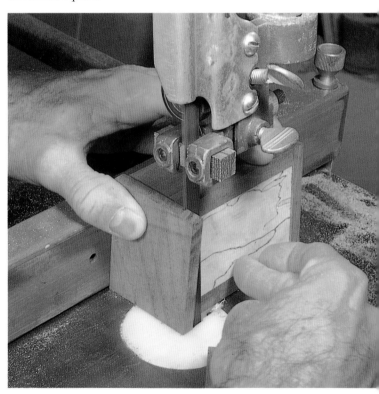

Set the band saw table at the same angle used to cut the lids, and cut the ends to match the shape of the top.

STEP 17
Final Finish
Orbital sand all sides of the boxes with a progression of grits from 180 to 240 and 320. With each sanding, gently round the front edge, sanding the corners as well as the flat surfaces. Use a holder clamped to the workbench to avoid the fatigue of using a large orbital sander. Finish the box with three coats of Danish oil.

Use a ¹⁄₁₆" roundover bit to route the front edge of the lid after sanding it on the belt sander.

ROUTER TABLE SAFETY

One of the things that make the router a relatively safe tool is that generally, while it's in use, both hands are placed firmly on its handles. When using a router inverted in a router table, it becomes infinitely more dangerous unless special care is taken in setting up guards to keep the fingers out of the way of the moving router bit. Because I use the router for so many diverse operations, it is not practical to have a safety guard that is useful in all the various set-ups. I have found it fast and convenient to make safety blocking from various pieces of scrap wood clamped in place on the surface of the router table. The router table becomes even more dangerous when using a technique called "climb feeding," which means that the router is turning in a direction that "self-feeds"—like a radial arm saw—pulling the wood into the cut. This technique can give a smoother cut with less likelihood of tear-out, but at greater risk to you, since the router bit can grab the wood and pull it (and your fingers) into the cut. The tendency to—climb feed—is reduced when cutting end grain and soft woods and is proportionate to the size of the cut. The danger increases with a dull router bit cutting along the grain, or on particularly hard pieces of wood, like figured walnut. It is extremely important in all cases to use safety blocking to prevent serious injury when making a "climb feed" cut.

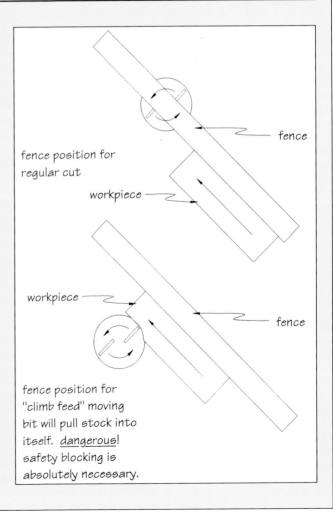

fence

fence position for regular cut

workpiece

workpiece

fence

fence position for "climb feed" moving bit will pull stock into itself. <u>dangerous</u>! safety blocking is absolutely necessary.

The Checkerboard Inlay Box

This box is made of curly sugar maple with inlay of walnut and fiddleback soft maple. It is a good size to use as a collection point for all the stuff that collects in your pockets during the day: pens, pencils, pocket knives, keys and so on. Its angled ends and sides and the checkerboard inlay give it a very contemporary look. Its mortise-and-tenon craftsmanship will allow it to last through many years of use. The angled resawing technique uses materials efficiently.

MAKING THE BOX

STEP 1

Resaw the Stock

While the outside of this box consists of angled planes, the inside shape is rectangular, with 90° sides. To make this box, resaw wood on the band saw for the sides and ends at a 9 or 10° angle. The exact degree of the angle is not critical to the success of this project. Mark out the shape of the box end on the end of the board, tilt the band saw table to align with that mark, cut into the end of the stock and turn it over to see that the saw is cutting into the exact center. If not, adjust the fence in or out as necessary. If 5/4 stock is not available, plan your cutting so that parts overlap, keeping waste at a minimum. This requires wider stock to form the parts, but is still thrifty when using fine woods. To figure the size of stock needed, sketch out the shape of the resawn, finished-size stock, cut out two pieces of paper in that shape and slide them in relation to each other until they fit within the thickness of the stock, allowing ³⁄₁₆″ between them for the band saw kerf and cleanup allowance. Use the same angle to resaw the stock for the fronts and backs of the box, but you can use narrower stock to come out with the right width for these parts.

STEP 2
Sand the Resawn Pieces
After the stock is resawn, run it through a tapered disk sander on the table saw to cut down on your sanding time later and to remove the band saw marks.

STEP 3
Lay Out the Mortises on the End Pieces
The ends are not cut to final shape until they have been machined to fit the other parts. Cut them to length, as shown in the drawing at bottom right, and then lay out the exact positions of the mortises for the front, back and bottom pieces. This is done with a sliding T-bevel, a pencil and a square. The angled lines shown are transferred from the shape of the angled stock, using the sliding T-bevel.

STEP 4
Cut the Mortises
To form the mortises in this box, use the same procedure described for mortising the ends of the walnut box with spalted maple inlay in chapter eight, with the following differences. Set the height of the ⅛″ cutter at ³⁄₁₆″ above the router table. Check with a dial caliper when making a test mortise. I am satisfied with the depth when it is just over ¹²⁄₆₄″. Set the fence so that the position of the mortise will allow for waste to be trimmed from the end pieces after assembly.

Route the mortises for the front and back pieces first; these require the same fence setting, but different settings for the stop blocks. Then adjust the fence to cut the mortise for the bottom panel to fit, cutting between the mortises you have already cut for the front and back.

MATERIALS LIST		
5/4 Curly sugar maple		3″ × 16″
Brass pins	2 pcs.	³⁄₁₆″ (cut from brass welding rod)
Ends	2 pcs.	3⅝″ × 3″
Sides	2 pcs.	1¾″ × 6⅜″
Bottom	1 pc.	⅛″ × 2¼″ × 6⅜″ (birch plywood)
Top	1 pc.	½″ × 2⅝″ × 6″ (before final trimming)

TOOLS LIST	
Band saw	Table saw
Jointer	Planer
Router table	Orbital sander
⅛″ roundover bit	⅛″ and ¾″ or 1″ straight-cut bit
Stationary belt sander	45° chamfering bit
	Tapered sanding disk

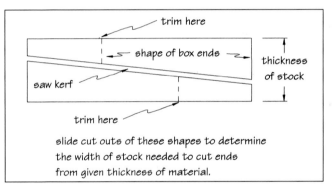

slide cut outs of these shapes to determine the width of stock needed to cut ends from given thickness of material.

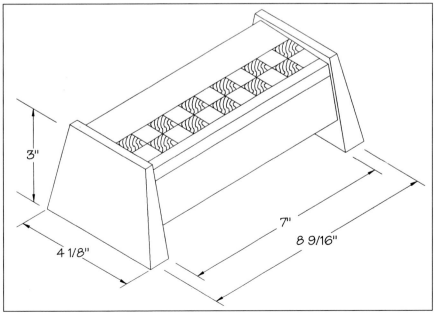

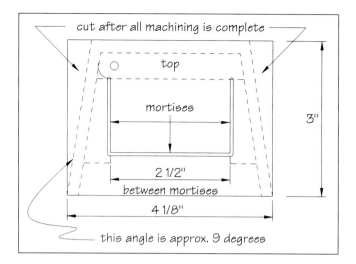

cut after all machining is complete

top

mortises

3"

2 1/2"
between mortises

4 1/8"

this angle is approx. 9 degrees

A run through your disk sander will cut down on sanding time later.

STEP 5
Cut the Tenons for the Front and Back Pieces

Cutting the tenons for the front and back pieces to fit the end mortises is done exactly as for making the walnut box with spalted inlay (chapter eight), except that the tenon is cut to the *exact* length of ³⁄₁₆″. Check the length of the tenon with the dial indicator. I am satisfied when it reads exactly ¹²⁄₆₄″. Take special care cutting the tenons, due to the added thickness and shape of the front and back pieces, and fix safety blocks on the router table to keep your fingers clear of the cutter.

STEP 6
Finish the Tenons

Cut the dadoes in the front and back pieces for the bottom panel to fit using the table saw with the blade height set to ⅛″ and the distance of the blade from the fence at ⅛″. Then cut the remaining nubs from the ends of the front and back pieces using the sliding cutoff table with a stop block to guarantee the cut conforms to the routed cut forming the tenon.

STEP 7
Make the Bottom

Cut the bottom from ⅛″ Baltic birch plywood, checking the fit of the plywood in the mortises. If they are too tight, use the straight-cut bit in the router to size the stock to fit into the mortises in the end pieces while the router table is still set up from making the tenons. (Details of this procedure are described in chapter eight.)

STEP 8
Shape the Ends

After the machining operations on the ends are complete, set up the saw to trim the ends to final shape. I use a

Using a square and a sliding T-bevel, mark the mortises and the cut lines on a sample end piece, and route the mortises in the same way end pieces are formed for the walnut box with spalted maple inlays in chapter eight.

sliding cutoff table on the table saw which, unlike the normal cutoff table, does not have a fixed fence and allows simple cutting of complex shapes.

STEP 9
Make the Channel for the Inlay

Route the channel for the inlay to fit while the lid is still oversize in width and length, using the procedures described in chapter one. In this box, the inlay provides a point of reference that indicates where to open the box, so route the channel on the side rather than centering it. A single narrow band placed in the center of the lid would lose its significance, and a wide band would hide too much of the curly pattern on the top.

After routing the mortises, cut the end pieces to shape using the cutoff table on the table saw with a guide strip tacked in place. The sliding T-bevel is very useful for setting up the desired angle.

To determine the finished size of the top, assemble the box and mark the cut lines to trim the front and back edges at the angle that matches the front and back pieces, and then cut the lid to length to fit within the space allowed by the ends.

STEP 10
Dry-Assemble the Box and Trim the Top

After the inlay is complete and the clamps are removed, assemble the box without glue, measure the completed space between the ends and cut the top to fit the measured length. Check the fit: If it is tight, meaning that there is no side-to-side movement at all, then cut just a tiny bit more off on the table saw. Using the cutoff box works very well for this. First, you know that the piece will come out square, and second, when using a stop block, it is very easy to cut off just the right amount. Move the workpiece over until you see a very slight space, and then, holding the workpiece firmly in position, re-clamp the stop block against the workpiece.

MAKING THE HINGES

STEP 1
Bore Holes in the Top

This box uses a ³⁄₁₆″ brass welding rod as hidden hinge pins. To form the hinges, drill ³⁄₁₆″ holes in the ends of the lid. I use my old Shop Smith as a horizontal boring machine, using a ³⁄₁₆″ drill and tilting the table parallel. To drill these holes with a conventional drill press, you could construct a jig to hold the stock on the table parallel to the bit, as shown in the drawing below. Raise the table so that the drill will be centered in the workpiece. Set up a guide block to position the hole exactly where you want it, and use the fence to hold the workpiece in position. Drill a test piece, and check the location of the hole with the dial indicator. Drill to a depth of about ³⁄₈″, about ¹¹⁄₆₄″ from the back edge and the inside surface of the top. Then set up the same arrangement to drill the other end of the top, once again testing the position of the hole with a test piece.

STEP 2
Route the Back Edge and Cut the Angles in the Lid

Route the back edge of the lid with a ¼″ roundover bit to give the lid clearance for opening. Then cut the lid to match the angles of the front and back pieces. Set up the saw, transferring the angle from the box front with the sliding T-bevel to set the angle of the saw blade. First trim the back edge to shape, taking care not to cut into the

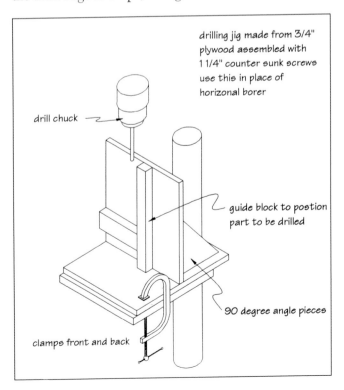

drilling jig made from 3/4" plywood assembled with 1 1/4" counter sunk screws use this in place of horizontal borer

drill chuck

guide block to postion part to be drilled

90 degree angle pieces

clamps front and back

Use a horizontal borer for drilling the pin holes in the top. You can also use a jig on the drill press as shown in the drawing.

Drill holes for the hinge pins to fit into the ends with a ³/₁₆″ brad-point bit. The opposite end, reversed and placed underneath, holds the workpiece square to the drill without changing the angle of the drill press table.

portion of the back edge shaped by the ¼″ roundover, and then cut the front edge. An easy way to determine where to cut is to lay the lid in place on the dry-assembled box, use a straightedge to align the lid with the box back and then use a pencil to mark a cut line along the front edge of the lid.

STEP 3
Drill Hinge-Pin Holes in the End Pieces
To drill the hinge-pin holes in the end pieces, first locate the positions for the holes while the box is dry assembled. Use a steel rule laid against the angled back and mark the angle on the inside of the ends. Use this marking as a point from which to measure the location for the hinge-pin holes to be drilled, remembering to allow ¹/₃₂″ clearance between the lid and box back for the lid to open. Use a matching piece with the same angle, reversed, to hold the end piece in proper relation to the drill.

MAKING THE HINGE PINS
STEP 1
Cut the Brass to Length
Cutting the brass hinge pins can be done with a hacksaw, but because I usually cut the pins for several boxes at a time, I use an old carbide blade in the table saw and the sliding cutoff table. Set the stop block a distance from the blade determined by adding the depth of the hinge hole in the end pieces and the depth of the holes drilled in the tops, less ¹/₆₄″. Lower the blade so that it does not cut all the way through the rod, leaving just a little to break off by hand. This helps avoid having the piece break off while being cut and consequently being thrown by the saw. (I wear a face shield while cutting the pins just in case this should happen.)

STEP 2
Clean Up the Pin Ends
After the pins are cut to length, sand the ends by rolling the pins against the stationary belt sander with your fingers. This step helps the box assembly go more smoothly.

FINISHING TOUCHES
STEP 1
Route the Edges
Route all edges with a 45° chamfering bit. Use the same setting to route the ends and bottom edges of the front and back. Lower the bit to route a smaller chamfer on the top edges of the front and back. Use a ⅛″ roundover bit to route the inside edges of the front and back.

STEP 2
Sanding
Sand all the parts of this box prior to assembly, proceeding through the usual sequence of grits: 180, 240 and 320. Use an orbital sander inverted in a holder mounted on the workbench to make this job easier. The small chamfered edges are much easier to sand by hand with a sanding block: This will avoid unintended rounding of edges, keeping the lines of the box crisp and clean.

FINAL ASSEMBLY
STEP 1
Install the Hinge Pins in the Lid and Glue Up the Front and Back
After placing the hinge pins in the lid, apply glue with a squeeze bottle to the insides of the end mortises, and then

put the front, back, bottom pieces and lid in place on one end. Using a piece of folded-over business card stock, shim the opposite end of the lid in position and place the other end piece in place. If your tenons are cut just right, the box will hold together without clamps.

STEP 3
Check the Fit of the Lid
Check that the box is square by opening and closing the lid and observing its fit. If the lid rubs on one side, squeeze it from corner to corner, and check the lid operation again. If necessary, clamp the box together, using cushion blocks cut at the same angle as the sides and fronts to give even clamping pressure.

STEP 4
Finish the Box
Finish the box in the usual manner with three coats of Danish oil.

After routing all the pieces and sanding each one to 320-grit, put glue in the mortises and assemble the box. Opening and closing the lid will indicate if the box is square and clearances are adequate.

CREATIVITY

While it has been said that there is nothing new under the sun, we do witness occasional rearrangements. These rearrangements may appear to come from out of the blue for those observing from outside the creative process. For example, here in Eureka Springs we have a small roadside chapel built on a wooded hillside, called Thornecrown Chapel. It was designed by an Arkansas architect, E. Faye Jones, and has received many of the most prestigious architectural awards, including the AIA Gold Medal. To reach Thornecrown Chapel, you must get out of your car and follow a pathway through the woods past limestone outcroppings, and between slender oaks and pines. The chapel's structure, stained only a shade lighter than the bark of the surrounding trees, lifts the walls of glass nearly to the height of the trees' towering canopy.

Every element is familiar, and yet the way the elements are put together is new and inspirational. In looking at Thornecrown Chapel from outside the context of E. Faye Jones's career as an architect, the sources of design are nearly incomprehensible. But as I became aware of the other buildings designed by Mr. Jones, I began to see a pattern in the use of elements of design leading to the creation of Thornecrown Chapel. It is clear that Thornecrown Chapel is a high point in a creative process.

If you study the careers of other artists, you find

creative process—movement leading from finished work to finished work, each building upon or expanding themes and concepts expressed in earlier work. We woodworkers tend to think of ourselves as "making things," rather than observing ourselves as part of a creative process. To become "creative" involves a shift from thinking about objects and products to the more subjective reality of process. One of the factors that has enabled me to do quality work has been a focus directed beyond immediate projects toward long-term growth as a woodworker. I look at projects as opportunities for building necessary technical and design skills, as well as an opportunities to express my innermost values. I like to discuss with my customers the merits of various joinery techniques and direct the design of a project toward giving me the opportunity to learn what most interests me. This process not only gives me the growth opportunities I look for, but gives the customer a conscious role in my growth as a craftsman and more involvement in the creative process.

In starting the creative process, the artist or craftsman asks the question, "What is most important to me?" and then begins a search directed toward expressing his or her essential values. It is a process of learning and growth that leads us consciously within, to deeper levels of understanding of ourselves and our relationship to the outside world.

CHAPTER 10

Sculpted Pecan Box

This box, with its secret drawer, sculpted pecan lid and walnut pull, is very similar in its construction techniques to the box in the previous chapter: It is constructed with mortise-and-tenon joints. It differs in that the checkerboard inlaid box is finish sanded prior to assembly, while this one is sanded after. The inspiration for this box comes from the hills and valleys surrounding my home in the Ozark Mountains. Our forest takes its shape from the underlying landscape, which is more clearly revealed in early November when the leaves fall. The Ozark Mountains are not mountains in the technical sense, like the Rockies or the Appalachians, but have been formed through erosion—by the movement of water on a huge plateau over millions of years. I form the shape of the lid by "eroding" hollows from the central plateau of the pecan lid with the belt sander. This very imprecise operation depends on the skill and vision of the craftsperson.

MAKING THE BOX

I make this box with walnut ends and sides, and use pecan for the lid. This is an excellent use for figured wood, or even "disfigured" wood that displays knots and other imperfections.

STEP 1
Resaw the Walnut Stock

While the outside angles of the box are approximately 9°, the inside shape is rectangular, with 90° sides. To make this box, resaw wood on the band saw at about a 9° angle for the sides and ends. Use the same techniques to shape the sides and ends of this box as used to make the checkerboard inlay box in chapter nine. All of the parts for this box can be resawn at the same time or, to save material, the front and back pieces can be cut from narrower stock. After the stock is resawn, use a sanding disk on the table saw to bring the resawn stock to its finished dimension as shown in the previous chapter.

STEP 2
Route the Mortises

To form the mortises in this box, use the same procedure described for mortising the ends of the walnut box with spalted maple inlay, with the following differences. Set the height of the ⅛″ cutter at ³⁄₁₆″ above the router table. When making a test mortise, check with a dial caliper; I am satisfied with the depth when it is just barely over ¹²⁄₆₄″. Set the fence so that the position of the mortise will allow for waste to be trimmed from the end pieces after assembly. Use the same fence setting to route the mortises for both ends of the box, but change the positions of the stop blocks for routing the opposite sides and opposite ends—a total of four separate setups. The left and right ends of this box are different: One end has a secret drawer and the other does not. Adjust the fence to cut the mortises for the bottom panel: A single setup will cut the mortises for both ends if indexed from the top edge.

STEP 3
Cut the Tenons

Cutting the tenons for the front and back pieces to fit the end mortises is done exactly as for making the walnut box with spalted inlay, except that the tenon is cut to the *exact* length of ³⁄₁₆″ to fit the mortise cut for it. Using a test piece,

MATERIALS LIST		
5/4 walnut		3″ × 12″
Figured pecan		¾″ × 3⅜″ × 6″
Baltic birch		⅛″ × 6¼″ × 7″ (for box and drawer bottoms)
Sugar maple		A few sq. inches (for drawer sides)
Ends	2 pcs.	3″ × 4″
Front and back	2 pcs.	2¼″ × 6⅜″
Top	1 pc.	¾″ × 3⅜″ × 6″
Bottom	1 pc.	⅛″ × 3″ × 6⅜″
Drawer		
Bottom	1 pc.	⅛″ × 3⅛″ × 6 ³⁄₁₆″
Sides	2 pcs.	⁵⁄₁₆″ × ½″ × 5¹⁵⁄₁₆″
Back	1 pc.	⁵⁄₁₆″ × ½″ × 2¹¹⁄₁₆″

TOOLS LIST	
Table saw	Band saw
Router table	Drill press
Stationary belt sander	Orbital sander

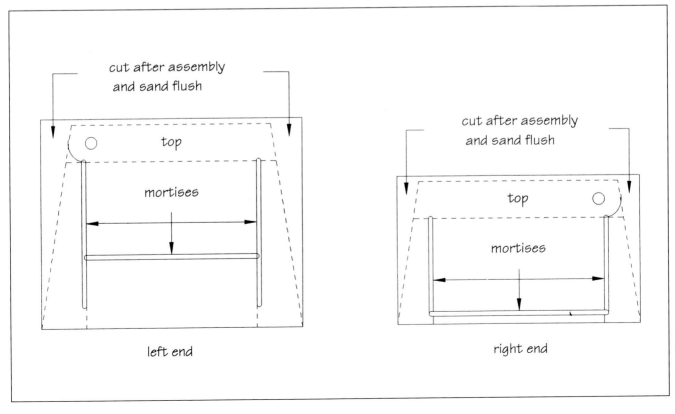

cut after assembly and sand flush

top

mortises

left end

cut after assembly and sand flush

top

mortises

right end

check the length of the tenon with the dial caliper, making sure it reads exactly $^{12}/_{64}''$. As in making the checkerboard inlay box, take special care in cutting the tenons, due to the added thickness and shape of the front and back pieces, and fix safety blocks on the router table to keep your fingers clear of the cutter.

STEP 4
Cut for the Drawer and Bottom to Fit
Use the table saw with a $^1/_8''$ blade raised to cut $^1/_8''$ deep to cut saw kerfs for the bottom panel to fit. To cut for the secret drawer to fit, raise the blade to $^3/_{16}''$ and change the position of the fence.

Next, trim away the nubs to allow the front and back pieces to fit the mortised ends. The drawing at bottom right shows the cuts for the bottom and drawer guide, and where to trim the nubs.

STEP 5
Make and Install the Hinges
Like the checkerboard inlay box, this box uses a $^3/_{16}''$ brass welding rod for hidden hinge pins. To drill the ends of the lid for the hinge pins to fit, use the procedures described in chapter nine, and then route the inside back edge with a $^1/_4''$ roundover bit to clear for opening the lid. Drilling the hinge-pin holes in the ends follows the same procedures used in making the checkerboard inlay box, except that you determine the locations for the hinge holes differently. First set up the top-to-bottom distance, allowing $^1/_{32}''$ for clearance in opening, and index the position of the hole from the top edge of the box. To determine the location for stop blocks to further position the holes, place the back piece in the mortise provided for it and, with a steel rule, follow the angle of the back, marking a line on the end piece to indicate the location of the back edge of the top after assembly. Measure the space between the holes in the ends of the lid and the back edge of the lid using the dial caliper. Use that distance to mark a line on the ends, measuring from the line of the angle of the back. This gives the outside position of the hole for the hinge pin to fit the lid. It is necessary to adjust the angle of the drill press table to compensate for the angle of the ends, or to use a matching piece with the same angle, reversed, to hold the end piece in proper relation to the drill. This simpler approach requires less setup time and leaves the table at 90° for other uses. Once you have set up to drill one end accurately, it is easy to set up for the opposite end using the technique shown on the next page.

Use the cutoff box to trim the tenons on the front and back pieces. Note that these tenons are cut to allow for the hidden drawer.

This shows the parts mortised, tenoned and nearly ready to assemble.

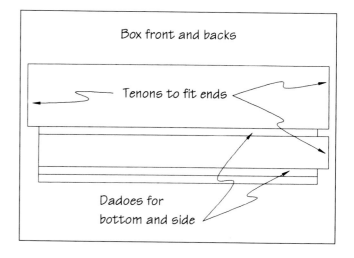

Box front and backs

Tenons to fit ends

Dadoes for bottom and side

Shape the Lid

Use the jig on the band saw that you used to cut the radius in the bracelet box top (chapter seven) to first give the lid a curved shape. Then alter the shape by "sculpting" it on the stationary belt sander. This is not a precise operation. It helps to adjust the belt sander to a comfortable working height, and to get a good secure body stance before starting. This is a risky operation in that a small slip can give unintended results. A comfortable body position is the first step in reducing risk.

STEP 7

Dry-Assemble the Box

First assemble the box without glue, allowing you to sand the front and back edges prior to fitting the walnut pull on the lid. Use the band saw, set at the same angle as the sides, to cut the end pieces and lid roughly to shape. Next, sand the surfaces flush on the stationary belt sander.

STEP 8

Attach the Pull

Attach an angled fence to the fence on the router table to hold the box lid at the correct angle to the 1/8" straight cutter, and use stop blocks to control the length of cut. Adjust the depth of cut of the router table to be just a tiny bit deeper than the tenon on the end of the pull to allow for finish sanding and gluing.

MAKING THE SECRET DRAWER

This box is a production item in my shop, and I keep the drawer simple so that all the drawers in the many boxes I make will work smoothly without a lot of fooling around. The drawer bottom serves double duty by acting as drawer guides. The drawer sides are glued and nailed to the drawer bottom, and the drawer front is made of the same walnut as the ends for color and grain match.

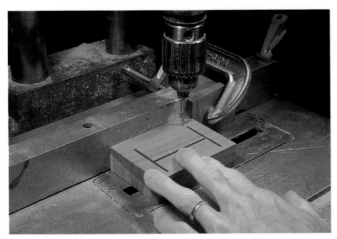

Drill for the hinge pins; use a matching piece to level the workpiece with the drill press. The stop block helps to accurately index for drilling the opposite end as shown in the next photos.

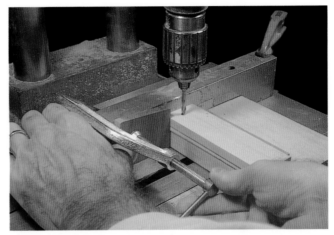

Drill a piece of scrap wood clear through, and then turn it over and use it to set up the stop block for drilling the opposite end of the box.

Now drill the holes in the opposite ends.

Shaping the sculpted top on the belt sander.

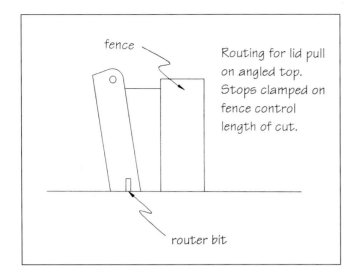

fence

Routing for lid pull on angled top. Stops clamped on fence control length of cut.

router bit

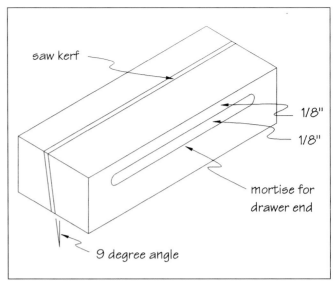

saw kerf

1/8"

1/8"

mortise for drawer end

9 degree angle

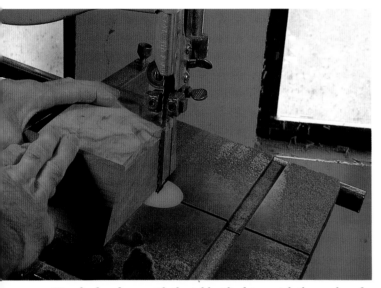

Use the band saw with the table tilted to match the angles of the sides to trim the box ends and lid.

Pull the trial-assembled box apart and, with an angled guide piece clamped to the router table fence, set up stops and route the front edge of the lid with a ⅛" straight-cut bit for the small walnut pull to fit.

STEP 1
Make the Drawer Face
To make the drawer face, cut a piece of walnut to match the angle of the sides by resawing the piece into angled strips, as shown above. Cut the angled strips to the same length as the box ends and, with the ⅛" straight-cut bit in the router, cut the mortise for the box bottom to fit using the same technique as in making the ends, and using the drawer guide slots cut in the front and back of the box to determine the position of the fence. Index this cut from the top edge of the drawer front, and make an extra for the inevitable trial and error involved in getting a good fit.

STEP 2
Make the Drawer Sides
Resaw sugar maple and plane it to size. Then, using the mitered cutoff table on the table saw, cut mitered corners on the parts, cutting the drawer back to exact size and leaving the sides long to be cut to equal length using the 90° cutoff table on the table saw, with a stop block to be certain they are uniform in length.

STEP 3
Assemble the Drawers
Make a jig to hold the side pieces in place while the bottom is glued and nailed in place with slight-headed brads. To assemble the drawer, first glue the box bottom in the mortise cut in the drawer front; lay the side and back pieces in the jig, squeeze a line of glue on the pieces, align the drawer bottom in place and then tack brads into place. After the glue has dried, drill a ⅛" hole through the center of the drawer back for the stop pin, which will be tacked into place when the box is completely finished.

Form the drawer by gluing parts to the Baltic birch plywood drawer bottom; use brads to give added strength.

FINAL ASSEMBLY AND FINISHING

STEP 1
Assemble the Box

Follow the same assembly procedures used in assembling the checkerboard inlay box, chapter nine, and as shown in the photo at bottom right.

STEP 2
Check for Square

Check to see that the box is square by opening and closing the lid and observing its fit. If necessary, clamp the box together, using cushion blocks cut at the same angle as the sides and fronts to provide even clamping pressure.

STEP 3
Sand the Box

With the drawer in place, sand the box on the stationary belt sander, starting out with 100-grit to sand the ends even with the sides and the drawer facing even with the end, and to sand the top edges of the ends even with contours of the lid. Then change belts to 150-grit, and repeat the sanding operation. Use the inverted orbital sander to sand the box through grits 180, 240 and 320.

STEP 4
Finish the Box

Apply the Danish oil finish to the box, with the drawer removed. I do two coats the first day, waiting about 30 minutes between coats and about an hour before rubbing out the finish with a clean, soft cloth. After about 24 hours, I apply a third coat, which I rub out when the surface starts to feel a little sticky. When the finish is completely dry, I tack a ⅛″ dowel pin in the hole in the drawer to serve as a drawer stop.

Assemble the box permanently with glue spread in the mortises. If the mortises and tenons fit perfectly, the box assembles without clamps. If necessary, use clamps and angled cushion blocks to hold the joints tight for gluing.

MAKING YOUR OWN BOX PULLS

The very small lift tabs used on the sculpted box and tea chest (chapter twelve) can be made easily and safely despite their small size. In making small parts, I like to do all the important steps while they are in a large enough form to be manageable.

STEP 1
Size the Pull Stock

Start by resawing a piece of walnut to about ¼″ thick and with the tapered sanding disk in the table saw, sand it down to about 3⁄16″ thick. Set up the router table with a 5⁄16″ straight cutter and make a cut on each side, about 1⁄32″ deep, leaving ⅛″ at the center. Position the fence so that the lift tab will be about ⅛″ high.

Begin forming the tenon on the walnut lift tab with a straight-cut router bit. The open space between the fence and bit determines the height of the lift tab.

CERTAINTY AND RISK

In his book, *The Nature and Art of Workmanship*, David Pye discussed what he viewed as two types of workmanship: that of certainty and that of risk. Tasks like those performed in modern manufacturing, where probabilities of success are high enough to be considered without risk of failure, he describes as being workmanship of certainty. Workmanship like cutting dovetails by hand where a slip of the chisel might mean failure involves workmanship of risk. The task of becoming a "better" woodworker is addressed by attempting to increase the certainties of one's work, either by changing the technology involved or by developing the level of skill of the woodworker. These are choices that woodworkers make every day in selecting our tools and processes. Our culture places so much emphasis on the products that come from woodworking, measuring them against the standards of the manufacturing industries, and tending to overlook that which is essential in their nature—that they are evidence of a process of personal growth and discovery. From my view, it is that process that is ultimately of greatest value. Many times, as I have shown my work in craft fairs, beginning woodworkers have come up to me, and while admiring my work, have been apologetic for their own. But woodworking, at its best, is not finished work. For me, the best projects have not necessarily been the ones that have come out the best. My best projects have been those that have challenged and inspired me to explore new areas in my work, to learn new skills and to tran-scend what I had thought were my limits. On this scale of measurement, the best workmanship must involve risk. All good design has been achieved through individual and collective effort of trial and error, meaning, of course, that it has evolved through continuing attempts to rectify and learn from the mistakes of the past. Workmanship, whether that of certainty or risk, has evolved through the process of trial and error as well. Unless a person is ready to risk failure, there is no point in beginning. I encourage you to make your very own mistakes without personal recrimination. I am a believer in the principle that crisis and opportunity are the same thing. When I make mistakes—and as a forty-hour-a-week professional, I make many (some of them *large*)—I have learned to look and listen for the opportunity presented to me to learn something, to improve my work or to practice forgiveness of myself, and occasionally the mistakes I make become the inspiration for new work. Because I work with wood for a living, and because my work must be produced and sold at a price people can reasonably afford, I have become dependent on the use of power tools for many of the operations involved in its production. This is not a bad thing. But the sound of a plane whispering in the ear is a far more engaging and satisfying sound than a router, and I hope that, as the meaning of craftsmanship becomes better understood for its cultural value, new opportunities will emerge for people to enjoy the quieter forms of the woodworking art.

Use a plunge type beading bit to form the rounded ends of the pulls.

Cut the pulls to length on the table saw, using a cutoff box.

STEP 2
Roundover the Sides
Use a ⅛″ roundover bit in the router to route both sides of the workpiece. Use a plunge type ⅛″ beading bit in the router to cut the roundovers on the ends of the pulls. Use a backing block to help hold the workpiece steady and vertical as it passes over the cutter.

STEP 3
Cut to Length
On the table saw, use the cutoff box to cut the lift tabs to length, cutting in at the flat spot left by the beading bit.

STEP 4
Cutting the Tenon on the Pull
With the lift tab on end, and using a stop block to position the cut, make a saw cut to define the tenon portion of the lift tab. With the cutoff box, cut the lift tab away from the walnut stock. To finish forming the tenon, make a final cut with the blade only barely raised above the table.

Cut the shoulders of the tenon on the table saw. The stop block accurately positions the cut.

Another small cut at each end prepares it to fit a ⅛″ routed mortise.

MAKING THE PULL FOR THE CHERRY JEWELRY BOX

I make this drawer pull from walnut, resawn and planed to a thickness of ⅜″. It can be very dangerous to work on tiny little pieces like these, so I work with a fairly long piece of walnut stock for most of these steps and leave the final cutoff of the finished pull for last. I make a template for shaping the knob from a piece of scrap hardwood of the same dimension as the planed size of the walnut stock. Using ony one end of the hardwood piece, I shape it to the profile of the finished pull, using the band saw and stationary belt sander.

STEP 1
Form the Tenons

The first step in making the pull is to form the tenon on the ends of the pulls using a ⁵⁄₁₆″ straight-cut router bit mounted in the router table, with a fence set up to control the location of the tenon. Adjust the height of the cutter so that after cutting on both sides, the remaining wood will measure ⅛″ thick. Use the dial indicator to check this dimension.

STEP 2
Route the Cove

Next, use a ½″ core box bit in the router table and adjust the location of the fence to route the cove shape on the top and bottom of the pull. This cove shape enables the fingers to get a good grip opening a door or drawer.

Use the ⁵⁄₁₆″ straight-cut router bit in the router table to begin forming the tenon in the walnut stock. Check with a dial caliper that the remaining stock measures ⅛″.

Use a ½″ core box bit in the router table to cut the cove in the top and bottom of the pull.

With the ¼″ dado blade in the table saw, I cut into each side of the workpiece to finish forming its tenon.

STEP 3
Trim the Tenon Shoulders

Using the cutoff box on the table saw and a ¼″ dado blade, trim the shoulders of the tenon to match the shoulders routed on the router table, narrowing the tenon, and enabling the rest of the pull to hide the outer edges of the mortise cut for the drawer guide to fit.

STEP 4
Shape the Outside of the Pulls

Now clamp the template tightly to the walnut stock and use it with a template-following router bit to shape the pulls. The final shaping is done with the router table and a ⅛″ roundover bit adjusted to cut flush with the table top. Use this router setup to finish shaping the pulls, cutting all around the edges on both sides. It helps in sanding the pulls for it to still be attached to the walnut stock.

STEP 5
Cut the Pull to Length

Cutting the pull free from the walnut stock is the final step, which you do with the cutoff box on the table saw.

Following the basic steps offered here can create pulls of various shapes and sizes from beautiful hardwoods. I used pulls made in this way for several of the projects in this book, using the chamfering bit to route the pulls for the earring chest in place of the roundover, to be in keeping with the chamfered raised inlay used in that project. For the CD cabinet and Rachel's jewelry cabinet, I made larger, more angular pulls to be more in keeping with the scale and design of those projects.

Use a template made of hardwood, and a template-following router bit to route the shape of the finished pull.

CHAPTER II

CD Cabinet

A small cabinet is an excellent use for figured and interesting woods that may only be available in small quantities. This CD cabinet is designed to hold sixty CDs, and is a practical object as well as a way to show fine native wood in its best light. The wood for the front panels of this cabinet was sold to me as elm by the sawmill that cut it, which only goes to show that even experts can be fooled, and that the variations within species of hardwoods can make their recognition difficult even for people who work with them every day. Elm usually has a lot of variation in tone, moving from warm, creamy tones into dark copper, with the grain strong and reflective. After selecting the elm for the top, bottom and sides of this cabinet, I discovered—using my nose as I pushed the lumber through the saw—that the "elm" panels for the front were actually pecan. The design of this cabinet is partially inspired by the simple lines of work by James Krenov, whose book, *A Cabinet Maker's Notebook*, gave me early inspiration and encouragement to pursue quality craftsmanship in my own work. I used the walnut inlay in the doors to visually shorten the overly tall and narrow doors, to catch and reflect the angles used in shaping the top and to bring the eye toward the walnut pulls, inviting the hand to open the cabinet for CDs.

BUILDING THE CARCASS

This cabinet is assembled using dowels to connect the top and bottom to the sides, with a routed dado at the back to house the 1/4″ plywood back panel.

STEP 1

Cut the Dadoes for the CDs

Use a dado blade in the table saw with a cutoff box to cut the dadoes in the cabinet sides and midsection. Set up a stop block to control the position of the cut, and cut each side and both sides of the midsection before changing the stop block for the next cut. This way, all the dadoes will be in perfect alignment with each other, even if you get a

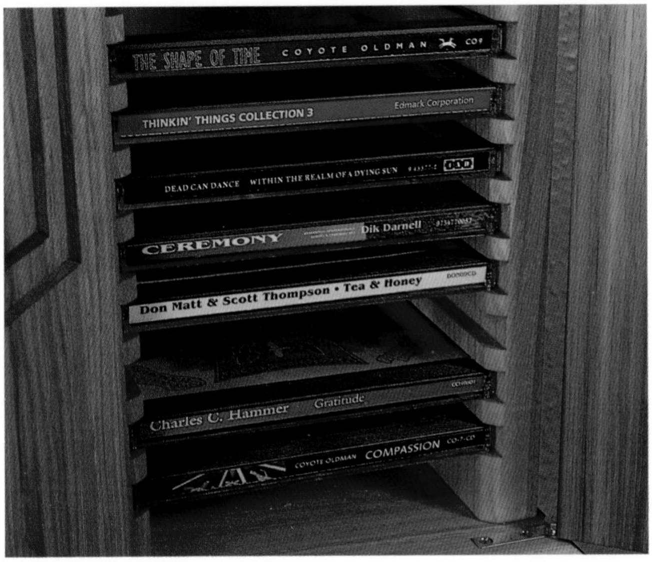

MATERIALS LIST

Elm		6 b.f. (for sides center divider, bottom and top)
Pecan		3 b.f. (for doors)
Birch plywood		2.5 sq. ft. × 1/4″ (for back panel)
Bullet catches	2 pcs.	1/8″
Brusso knife hinges	2 pr.	5/16″
Top and bottom	2 pcs.	7/8″ × 7 5/8″ × 12 5/8″
Sides	2 pcs.	13/16″ × 6 3/8″ × 23 7/8″
Midsection	1 pc.	3/4″ × 5 7/8″ × 23 7/8″
Doors	2 pcs.	3/4″ × 5 5/8″ × 23 3/4″
Dowels	20 pcs 10 pcs.	3/8″ × 1 1/4″ 1/4″ × 1 1/4″
Bullet catches	2 pcs.	1/4″ (with catch cups)
Hanger strips	1 pc. 1 pc.	5/16″ × 1 3/8″ × 10 1/8″ 5/16″ × 1 3/8″ × 9 11/16″
Back	1 pc.	1/4″ × 10 3/8″ × 24 3/8″
Thick walnut		A few sq. inches × 5/16″ (for door pulls)

TOOLS LIST

Table saw	Jointer
Planer	Plunge router
Router	Doweling jig
Dowel centers	Bar clamps
Chisels	Electric drill
Drill press	

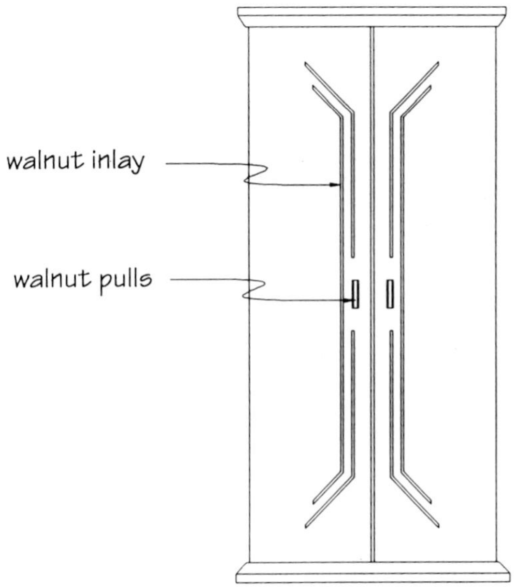

CD cabinet, closed

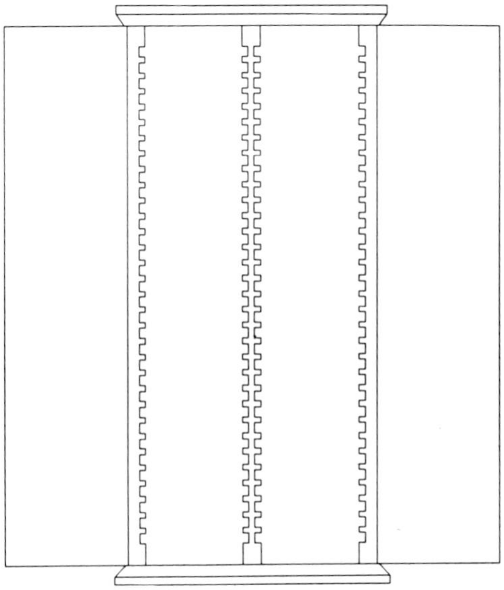

CD cabinet, open

When cutting the dadoes in the cabinet sides, a stop block clamped to the fence ensures accuracy of each cut.

Use spacer blocks clamped to the top and bottom pieces to accurately locate the positions of the sides and midsection; use dowel centers to mark the hole locations before drilling the matching dowel holes on the drill press.

bit off in your measurements between cuts. Use a stack-type dado blade with a ⁷⁄₁₆″ cut, and leave ⁵⁄₁₆″ between cuts. Leave a bit of extra space at the top and bottom so as not to intrude on the space needed for the dowels.

STEP 2
Drill Holes for Dowels

To attach the top and bottom to the midsection and sides, use a doweling jig and handheld electric drill. Use ⅜″ dowels for the sides and ¼″ dowels for the midsection. To mark the top and bottom for drilling on the drill press, use dowel centers, which are small, pointed, metal things designed to fit into particular-size holes and to indicate the position of the holes when the dowel centers are pressed into a mating piece of wood. To accurately position the sides, transferring the marks made with the dowel

centers, clamp blocks on the top and bottom—filling what will be the open spaces between the sides and midsection. This allows you to mark the dowel positions by simply pressing the side or midsection into place against the top. Because I only have one set of dowel centers, I move them between holes to mark the locations for drilling.

STEP 3
Chamfer the Edges

Route the edges of the top and bottom with a 45° chamfering bit in the router, routing deeper on the inside surfaces and taking only a shallow cut on the top and bottom edges. To keep these edges crisp, use a sanding block to sand them, and use the orbital sander on flat surfaces of the top and bottom and on the sides.

STEP 4
Cut the Panel for the Back

Use a ³⁄₁₆″ straight-cut router bit in the plunge router to route for the back panel to fit in the sides, top and bottom. This allows you to accurately size the ¼″ back panel to fit by cutting the edge on either the table saw or router table, passing the panel between the saw blade or straight-cut router bit and the fence.

STEP 5
Cut and Fit the Hanger Strips

Before assembly, cut and fit the hanger strip for the cabinet back and its matching wall piece. Cut the strips with a 15° angle. With one hanger strip leveled and screwed to the wall, and the other securely fixed to the back of the cabinet, these allow the cabinet to be easily hung or removed for cleaning by simply lifting it from the wall.

STEP 6
Install the Hanger Strip

After the back panel is cut to size and fitted to the carcass, glue the hanger strip in place. To accurately position it on the back panel, slip the back panel into the dado cut for it in the top. Spread glue on the hanger strip, clamp it on each end, with blocking on both sides to distribute pressure and prevent marking the stock, check with the dial calipers that there is an equal space at each end between the hanger end and panel end, and then, after removing it from the back, add additional C-clamps.

STEP 7
Install the Hinges

The mortises for the knife hinges and the holes for the bullet catches must be done before the cabinet can be assembled. Use the plunge router to cut the mortises for the knife hinges, using the router fence and pencil marks to guide the cut. (For a thorough explanation of how to install the knife hinges and bullet catches, please see chapter fourteen.)

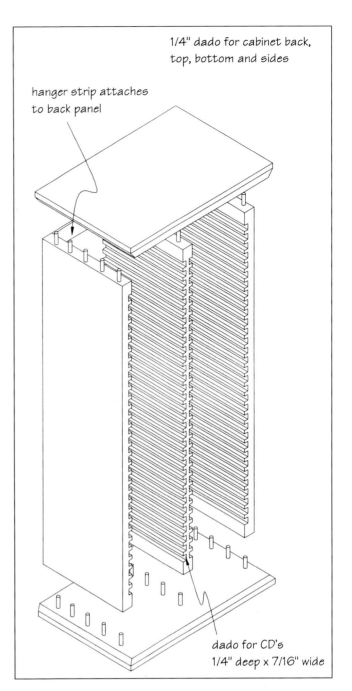

1/4" dado for cabinet back, top, bottom and sides

hanger strip attaches to back panel

dado for CD's
1/4" deep x 7/16" wide

The hanger strip with its 15° angle fits the matching wall hanger which will be attached to the wall. This piece must be glued in place before final assembly.

INLAYING THE DOORS

STEP 1
Lay Out the Design
To inlay the doors, first lay the design out in fine-line felt markers so that you can step back and be certain that you like the design as much on the wood as you did on paper. It's a good idea to look at the pattern from a variety of angles.

STEP 2
Cut the Channel
Use the plunge router with a ⅛″ carbide spiral-end mill to cut the clean edges of the routed channel. Route the channels parallel with the fence, and use clamped-in-place guide blocking to position the cut for the angled sections of inlay.

STEP 3
Clean Up the Channel
Use a small, straight chisel to finish the cuts, shaping the ends of the cuts to be consistent with the overall design.

STEP 4
Make the Inlay Strips
Make the inlay strips for this project using the technique shown in making inlay for Rachel's jewelry cabinet (chapter fourteen). Use a straight chisel to cut the inlay strips to the necessary angles, using a trial-and-error approach. Mark the angle by placing the strip partially into the channel and marking the cut line with the straight chisel. Remove the strip from the cabinet door before using the chisel to cut through the strip on the workbench.

STEP 5
Inlay the Strips
Use C-clamps, with cushion strips to distribute clamping pressure, when you glue the inlay strips in place. Sand the inlay strips flush to the surface of the cabinet doors after the glue has dried.

FINAL ASSEMBLY

STEP 1
Sanding
Before assembly, sand all the parts of the cabinet thoroughly, and use a sanding block to sand the sharp edges left after dadoing the sides and midsection.

Mark the inlay patterns on the door before deciding on the exact pattern you will use.

Square off the ends of the router cuts with a small chisel.

Lay the strips in place and precisely mark the ends with a chisel before cutting it to size.

This is the setup I use for routing the mortises for the knife hinges.

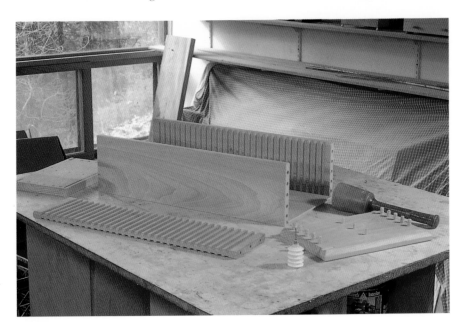

Lay out the pieces in the proper order for assembly.

STEP 2
Glue and Clamp the CD Cabinet
Lay the cabinet parts out in order for assembly, placing the cabinet back between the cabinet sides. The dowels are inserted in the top and bottom and glued. After putting glue in the mating dowel holes in the sides and midsection, use clamps and cushion blocks to pull the top and bottom into place, securely fitting the sides. Use the plunge router to route the door fronts for the door pulls.

STEP 3
Finishing
Use a Danish oil finish to bring out the natural beauty of the wood.

CHAPTER 12

The Tea Chest

I made my first tea box for a friend's fine restaurant: It was inlaid with burled walnut and curly maple cows grazing on a field of Ozark mountain cherry. Sometimes we are drawn to a project by the challenges it offers, and then discover that even though we are successful in a project, the work itself does not continue to interest us. That kind of sums up my relationship with the type of inlay known as *marquetry*. Because I have done a lot of inlay over the years, I am often asked to do this type of work. It is important for us, as woodworkers, to discover the kinds of work that we most enjoy and to follow the path that our pleasure outlines for us. From the inlay patterns I have developed and the boxes I have designed, you can see that I am most drawn to simple and elegant lines. I am most at home letting the wood do the talking.

I think of the phrase "working with wood" as describing a partnership agreement. The important word in the phrase is *with*. The craftsman and the wood contribute equally to the finished piece.

This tea chest is made from a very special and prized piece of crotch-figured walnut (from the intersection of tree limbs) and a very simple inlay of fiddleback maple and cherry. This box is made with the *box joint* (from the days of finely crafted cigar boxes). In those days, cigar boxes with this joint were described as having "locked" corners, and were associated with quality cigars—cigars worth going to greater expense to package. This joint is now more commonly known as the *finger joint*. I use a jig on the router table to cut the fingers and hollows for the box joint but, because I want inlay on the top edges, the final fingers are mitered on the table saw. This allows me to complete the inlaying of the box before it is assembled. I use a solid carbide spiral-end mill bit in the router to get a very clean cut. I designed the tea chest to hold various packaged teas in nine compartments. The size and shape of the compartments, and the overall shape and size of the box are determined by the packaging of the various teas.

BUILDING THE BOX

STEP 1
Resaw the Box Sides

Use black walnut, which you can resaw on the band saw from 5/4 stock, for the sides. This allows you to form nearly perfect grain patterns around the perimeter of the box, with one resawn piece forming the front and right side, and the matching piece forming the back and left side. Plane the resawn stock to ⁷⁄₁₆″ thick before cutting it to the dimensions for the box.

STEP 2
Make a Jig for Locked Corners

To make the jig to cut the locked corners, take a piece of ¾″ birch veneer plywood about 12″ × 24″, and make two dado cuts in it about ¼″ deep by ¾″ wide, about 2″ in from each edge. This provides a track for the upper part to slide over the router bit. Cut this into two pieces: One, which forms the top of the jig, is about 8″ long; the other, longer one forms the base for attaching the router. Cut a second ¼″ × ¾″ dado about 4″ in from the edge of the upper jig

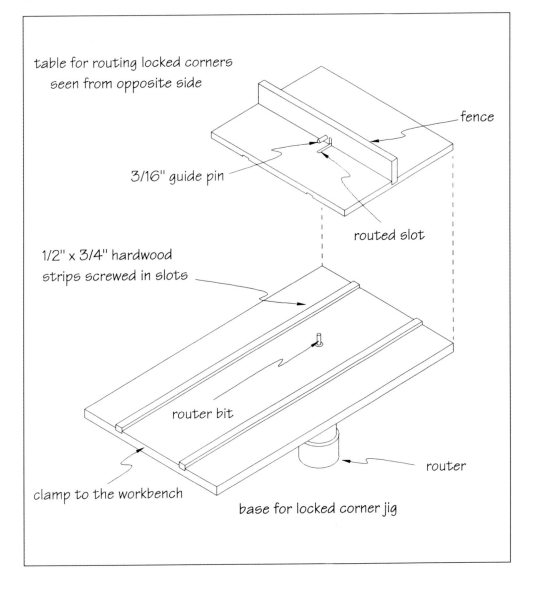

table for routing locked corners
    seen from opposite side

fence

3/16″ guide pin

routed slot

1/2″ x 3/4″ hardwood
strips screwed in slots

router bit

clamp to the workbench

base for locked corner jig

router

part and 90° to and on the opposite side of the first dadoes. In this dado attach a fence to hold the stock, and install screws from underneath to hold the fence in position. Attach runners in the dadoes of the base part of the jig, about ½″ × ¾″, so that it fits into the dadoes of the upper and lower parts. Use screws to attach these runners to the base section and machine screws to attach the router base to the underside of the lower unit. With a plunge-cutting bit in the router, and the lower unit clamped firmly to the workbench, turn on the router and gradually raise the cut until it passes up through the lower unit. Then repeat the procedure with a larger straight-cut router bit to cut the hole large enough for the collet of the router to enter the space, bringing the router bit closer to the workpiece. Then, with the bit to cut the locked corners in the router, put the upper part of the jig on the tracks and position it so that the router bit will, when raised, cut into the area just slightly ahead of the fence. Make the cuts in small increments, raising the bit a hair and sliding the upper part of the jig back and forth. Repeat this until the bit comes up through the surface with enough height to cut the length of the fingers required. I used a ³⁄₁₆″ brass pin as a guide pin to match the ³⁄₁₆″ carbide cutter used. To install the guide pin, I drilled a hole in the fence, about ³⁄₈″ from the bottom edge, so that it would be just high enough when installed in the jig to keep from collecting sawdust. With the guide pin in place, I cut test pieces to check the placement of the guide pin. If the fingers are too loose, I loosen the screws attaching the fence to the platform and nudge the fence slightly away from the cutter. Then I drill for a new screw in a new location to hold the fence in position. If the fingers are too tight, I nudge the fence slightly toward the cutter.

tween the guide pin and the first finger while you use a C-clamp to hold it firmly to the fence. This is to make the fingers of the fronts and backs "fit" the sides. Remove the shim before making the cut.

STEP 4
Make the Inlay for the Top

Inlay the top edges of the tea chest before the mitered corners are cut. The inlay is very simple, with a ³⁄₁₆″-wide strip of fiddleback maple laminated between two thin strips of cherry. Cut the cherry strips about ³⁄₃₂″ thick from ¾″ cherry stock, and glue them to the fiddleback maple, with blocks of solid wood on both sides to evenly distribute clamping pressure. After the glue has dried, joint one edge flush on the jointer. To bring the strips down to a uniform thickness of ⁵⁄₁₆″, use the tapered sanding disk in the table

Use a router table and spiral cutter to make the "locked" corners of the tea chest. The ³⁄₁₆″ brass pin from brass welding rod stock matches the diameter of the spiral cutter. Make the cuts, holding the front and back pieces against the fence and brass pin, lifting each piece over the pin for consecutive cuts.

STEP 3
Cut the Fingers

Index all the cuts from the bottom edge, cutting the sides first, and then the fronts and backs. In cutting the sides, start with the bottom edges up against the guide pin, and hold the workpiece tight against the fence while sliding the platform forward and back across the router bit. Position subsequent cuts by lifting the finished finger over the guide pin. On the side pieces, stop short of cutting all the fingers, leaving the last ones to be cut into a miter joint at the top. To cut the fingers for the fronts and backs, use a shim be-

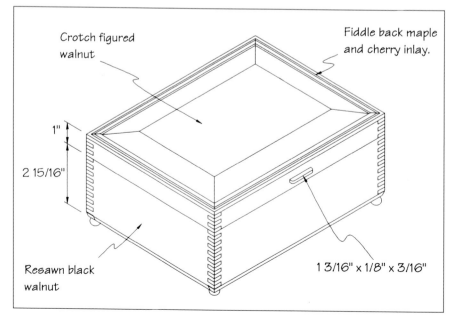

Crotch figured walnut

Fiddle back maple and cherry inlay.

1"

2 15/16"

Resawn black walnut

1 3/16" x 1/8" x 3/16"

Clamp the matching sides to the fence for the first cut, using an additional piece of brass rod for a spacer.

After the first cut is made, additional cuts follow the same procedure as for the front and back. To allow for the mitered corner, stop your cuts one cut short of the width of the side.

saw. This disk is used in place of a blade and, because the disk is tapered, it allows stock to be fed into it along the fence, with the abrasives cutting deeper as the stock moves toward the center of the disk. Because of the taper, the blade must be adjusted a bit off 90° to uniformly cut the strip top to bottom. (Use of the tapered sanding blade is shown in photographs in chapters nine and fourteen.) Cut a bit from each side of the strip until the cherry bands are each about 1/16" thick and, more importantly, the total width of the stock is 5/16" to match the width of the cutter for routing the inlay channel. Cut the inlay strips from this stock at about 1/8" thick to allow for the angle that will form in the top edges of the box parts.

STEP 5
Install the Inlay
To route for the inlay, use a 5/16" straight-cut router bit. Position the cutter to center the inlay in the stock, leaving about 1/16" of walnut on each side of the channel. Cut the inlay in lengths just barely over the lengths of the box parts, and glue them in place using blocking against the inlay to provide even clamping pressure.

STEP 6
Sand the Inlay Flush
After the glue has dried, use the tapered sanding disk to sand the inlay flush with the surrounding walnut so you will have a good square surface to cut the miters in the corners.

STEP 7
Miter the Side Pieces
Use the miter cutoff box to cut the corners on the sides, front and back. On the front and back pieces cut the miters clear through the top fingers, but on the side pieces lower the blade so that it cuts just enough away to allow the side to give clearance for the mitered finger to fit. Because the saw blade I use leaves a V cut, when cutting the sides to match, I lower the blade just enough to allow a small cleanup cut with a straight chisel.

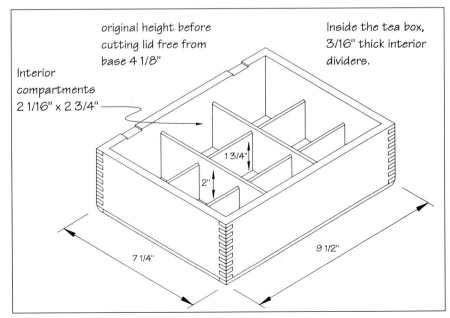

Interior compartments 2 1/16" x 2 3/4"

original height before cutting lid free from base 4 1/8"

Inside the tea box, 3/16" thick interior dividers.

1 3/4"

2"

7 1/4"

9 1/2"

Using a straight-cut bit in the router table, cut the channel for the inlay to fit. The inlay is made of fiddleback maple banded in cherry.

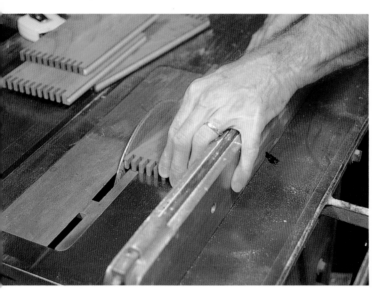

With the tapered sanding disk tilted to 90° in the table saw, sand the inlay flush with the top edges of the walnut sides.

Use the miter cutoff box on the table saw to cut the miters at the box corners. Rather than take time to change to a dado blade for the miters on the sides, I lower the blade to cut only what is neccesary for the corner to fit, and make several passes to cut away the waste.

STEP 8
Shape the Edges
Shape the top edges of the sides, front and back of the tea chest using the tapered sanding blade in the table saw. The object here is to provide a smooth transition into the angles that will be formed in the top panel. Check the ends of the parts to make sure you don't come close to sanding through the inlay.

STEP 9
Cut the Top Panel
Assemble the box to get the finished dimensions for the top panel, adding ⅜″ each direction to allow for the ³⁄₁₆″ × ³⁄₁₆″ tongues on the top panel, and subtracting ³⁄₃₂″ from the width for possible expansion and ¹⁄₃₂″ from the length to ease assembly. Cut the tongues on the panel and shape the top as shown below and top left, page 77.

STEP 10
Route Dadoes for the Top and Bottom
Use the router table and a ³⁄₁₆″ router bit to route for the top and bottom to fit. To avoid difficulties in assembling the box, plan the dado to house the top to correlate with the opening between fingers on the front and back. This will allow the top to slide in place after most of the interior elements of the box are in place during assembly. In order for the ¼″ birch plywood bottom to fit the ³⁄₁₆″ dado, use a straight-cut router bit and route the piece to fit.

The first cut to shape the edges of the top panel establishes the tongue depth.

The second cut defines the tongue length.

This final cut, with the blade set at 8°, establishes the shape of the panel.

STEP 11
Make the Interior Dividers

Make the interior dividers from ¾″ black walnut stock, resawn, planed and then sanded to ³⁄₁₆″ thick, using the tapered sanding disk. In order for the stock to fit into the rounded mortises, I route the top edges with a ⅛″ round-over bit. Note that the dividers running from front to back are taller than the side to side ones and require longer mortises. The procedure for setting up and routing for the dividers is shown on page 78.

STEP 12
Sanding

Before assembling the tea chest, sand all the interior parts, the inside surfaces of the sides, front and back, the inside and outside of the top panel, both sides of the bottom and the inlaid edges. Use a sanding block to sand the inside edges where the sides, front and back will intersect the top panel, and also the panel edges where they intersect the front, back and sides. This will visually soften the junction between these parts and give them more definition.

STEP 13
Assemble the Chest

Assemble the tea chest as a single unit, planning to cut the lid from the base after it is all glued together. An advantage of this method is that the top and bottom will align perfectly with each other. The disadvantage is that the interior parts can make assembly of a closed space challenging. Use blocks cut to size to hold the interior

With the start and stop points penciled on the router table fence, route the front, back and sides for the top panel and bottom to fit. Cut a test piece to check the position of the cut so that the bevel on the top comes out even with the beveled sides.

With a straight-cut bit in the router table, size the ¼″ plywood bottom panel to fit the ³⁄₁₆″ dadoes in the front, back and sides.

To route for the dividers, first route the mortise in the sides. Stop blocks ensure the mortise lengths will be the same for each piece.

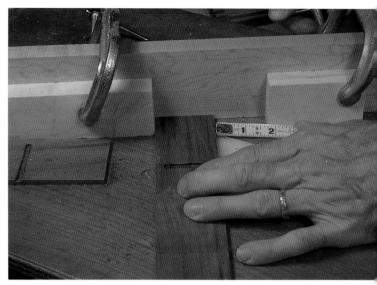

Next, I route the mortises in the dividers themselves.

The routed mortises in the dividers.

Routing a roundover on the top edge allows the dividers to fit the channels routed for them. Standing the pieces on edge keeps the pilot bearing in contact with the flat surface.

parts in place during assembly; to make the parts slip together easily, "sharpen" the interior parts slightly on the 6″ × 48″ belt sander.

STEP 14
Cut the Top From the Bottom
Use the table saw, with the blade raised just slightly above the 7/16″ thickness of the sides to make the cuts separating the top from the bottom. Because of the shape of the top, run the bottom of the box along the fence. After each cut, replace the saw kerf with a shim to hold the top and bottom in proper relation to each other and to prevent a miscut.

STEP 15
Clean Up the Cut
If the blade cuts well, and the fence is perfectly parallel to it, you may not need this step. Otherwise, clean up the saw cuts and make them even with a hand plane.

STEP 16
Install the Hinges
To assemble the box, use hinges that open only to 95°, eliminating the need for a lid support. Use a router to remove most of the waste from the hinge mortises. Carefully mark out the location for the hinges on the back edge of the top and bottom to make certain they are in perfect

Use spacer blocks, cut to the dimensions of the interior compartments, to hold the dividers in position during assembly.

Slide the top into place, and then the end, with glue spread on the matching fingers of the joint.

alignment. By using the router, you are able to get an accurate depth for the hinge mortises and better control of the tolerances between the lid and base of the box.

STEP 17
Install the Finger Pull
Use a small finger pull on the lid of the box to make it easy to open. Making this pull is described on page 63; I used the same pull, slightly shortened, on the sculpted box in chapter ten.

STEP 18
Shape the Sides of the Box
Use a hand plane to cut a very small chamfer on the outside edges of the top, and on the edges of the top and bottom where they intersect. Use the chamfering bit in the router table to route a slightly larger chamfer around the bottom edge, making it a bit more elegant and easier to pick up.

STEP 19
Finishing Up
I added small brass feet, which are glued in ⁵⁄₁₆″ holes in the corners, after sanding and applying the oil finish. The hardness of the crotch walnut panel enables it to take a tremendous finish that invites the touch.

As you make the cuts separating the top from the bottom, replace the saw kerf with shims and hold the box together with tape.

Use the router and straight-cut bit to route away most of the waste from the hinge mortise, leaving just a bit to clean up with the chisel.

CHAPTER 13

Jewelry Box With Hand-Cut Dovetails

Nothing expresses a craftsman's interest in quality as well as dovetails. To cut them by hand is a challenge for beginning woodworkers, offering satisfaction and self-confidence in reward. On this jewelry chest, I use a mitered dovetail on the top edge, which allows the use of a simple inlaid banding. Simple work, with emphasis on detail, can give a piece such as this lasting value. The sycamore used for inlay in the box is quartersawn, revealing its beautiful, soft, iridescent patterning. I use a great deal of cherry in the various pieces of furniture that I make, and the cherry parts for this box are leftovers and cutoff from a dining set. The dimensions of the box were determined in part by the size of the cherry panel I've used in the top.

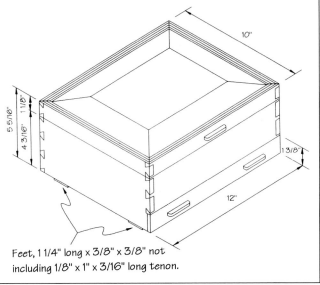

Feet, 1 1/4" long x 3/8" x 3/8" not
including 1/8" x 1" x 3/16" long tenon.

MATERIALS LIST

Cherry		⅝" (for sides, front, back and drawer front)
		¾" (for top)
		¾" (resawn to ⁵⁄₁₆" for the sliding compartments)
Cherry veneer plywood		¼" (for bottom)
Baltic birch plywood sliding compartment		⅛" (for drawer and tray bottoms)
4/4 Cherry		(to resaw for drawer sides)
Sides	2 pcs.	⅝" × 5⅜" × 10¹⁄₁₆"
Back	1 pc.	⅝" × 5⅜" × 12¹⁄₁₆"
Front	1 pc.	⅝" × 3¾" × 12¹⁄₁₆"
Top fill strips	2 pcs.	⅜" × ⅝" × 10¹³⁄₁₆"
	2 pcs.	⅜" × ⅝" × 8¹³⁄₁₆"
Top panel	1 pc.	¾" × 10½" × 8⅜"
Box bottom	1 pc.	11⅛" × 9¹⁄₁₆" × ¼"
Tray slides	2 pcs.	³⁄₁₆" × ¼" × 10¾"
Drawer guides	2 pcs.	³⁄₁₆" × ¼" × 8⅞"
Box dividers	2 pcs.	³⁄₁₆" × 1" × 9¹⁄₁₆"
Drawer parts		
Front	1 pc.	⅝" × 1⅝" × 12¹⁄₁₆"[1]
Sides	2 pcs.	⅜" × 1⅝" × 8¹⁵⁄₁₆"
Bottom	1 pc.	10¼" × 8⅝" × ⅛"
Tray parts		
Sides	4 pcs.	⁵⁄₁₆" × 1⅜" × 8¼"
Ends	4 pcs.	⁵⁄₁₆" × 1⅜" × 3⅝"
Dividers	6 pcs.	⅛" × 1" × 3¼"
Bottoms	2 pcs.	⅛" × 3¼" × 8¼"

[1]*Cut drawer front from same piece as box front.*

TOOLS LIST

Table saw	45° chamfering bit
Band saw	Planer
Router table	Dozuki (Japanese back saw)
Marking gauge	⅜" and ¼" chisels
³⁄₁₆" and ½" straight-cut router bits	Sliding T-bevel
	Chip-carving knife

MAKING HAND-CUT DOVETAILS

STEP 1
Lay Out Pins

Start this project by laying out the dovetails. Use a marking gauge to transfer the thickness of each cherry piece to the piece it will be joined with. Then use the sliding bevel, with the angle adjusted to an 8:1 ratio (the preferred angle for hardwood dovetails), to mark the tails on the side pieces. Lay out the dovetails, remembering to allow for the saw kerf when the top is cut away from the base of the box. Then use a chip-carving knife and a square to mark cut lines around the ends of the side stock.

STEP 2
Cut Out the Pins

Use the dozuki to follow your cut lines. A special feature of this box is the mitered dovetail used in the corners, which allows for the continuous inlay band around the perimeter of the top.

STEP 3
Allow for the Top Miter

Use the dozuki to help make the miter cut by cutting in only on the inside of the top corners.

STEP 4
Remove the Waste Between the Tails

Using the band saw, reduce chiseling time by removing some waste between the tails.

Use a marking gauge set about 1/32" over the thickness of the stock, a sliding T-bevel at a 1:8 ratio and a small square and pencil to lay out the dovetails, using the square to continue the markings around the corners.

Use the dozuki saw to cut the tails, following the pencil lines to where they intersect the line from the marking gauge, except for the tails in the top corners of the stock.

STEP 5
Clean Up the Tails

Now you can use the ¾″ straight chisel to clean up your dozuki saw cuts, and the ⅜″ straight chisel to remove the remaining stock between the tails. To finish the mitered dovetail at the corner, use the cutoff box on the table saw, with the blade raised almost to the height of the dovetail, allowing a small cleanup allowance for the chisel.

STEP 6
Lay Out the Pins

To cut the pins, position the tails so that you can use the knife to mark them directly where they will fit between

To cut the mitered dovetails for the top corners, follow the cut line on the inside, taking care not to cut through to the other side.

With a quick cut with a straight chisel, finish forming the mitered tail.

Use the mitered cutoff box on the table saw to cut the miter on the top corner of the sides, with the blade cutting a bit shy of the dozuki saw cut, leaving a little clean-up work for the chisel.

Lay the box side in position on the box back to mark it for cutting the pins. Use a knife to scribe the cut line, and then a small square to continue the cut lines down the face of the stock to meet the marking gauge line.

Then, use the dozuki saw again to follow the cut lines, being careful that the saw follows along the tail side of the pins.

After the pins and tails are cut with the dozuki saw, cut away some of the waste between the pins by using the band saw. With the workpiece face down, you can better avoid cutting into the pins by mistake. This step will speed up the cutting of the dovetails and by making the work easier, they will come out cleaner.

the pins. Use the square to continue the marks down the sides of the stock for the front and back.

STEP 7
Cut Out the Pins
Use the dozuki again to follow the cut lines, being careful that the saw follows along the tail side of the pins.

STEP 8
Cut Away the Waste Between Pins
Cut away some of the waste between the pins using the band saw. Make two cuts straight into the pin area, as shown above, and then two cuts at an angle to cut away the waste. Use a straight chisel to finish cutting the pins.

Then with straight chisels, remove the rest of the waste cutting along the marking gauge line from both sides of the stock. Clean up the pins and adjust them as necessary to fit the dovetails.

STEP 9

Miter the Top Pins

Before cleaning up the pins and tails to fit, use the mitered cutoff box on the table saw to cut the top pins on the front and back pieces to fit the mitered tails on the sides.

STEP 10

Clean Up the Sides and Fit

Clean up the pins and tails, adjusting them as necessary to fit. Then, when the box is pushed together for a test fitting, pry the box apart a little bit, take the dozuki and cut lightly into the miter. This cleans it up and gives a tight fit when the box is glued up.

After cutting the mitered top corners of the front and back on the table saw, assemble the box for a test fit and, with the joints open slightly, use the dozuki saw to cut into the miters, being careful not to cut into the dovetail itself. When the joints are pushed closed, the two sides of the miter will close to a perfect fit.

WOOD

Have you ever been to a hardwood lumber dealer and tried to find several matching boards for a project? I wondered why this was such a hard task until I watched the process of grading and sorting lumber at a large mill. A forklift truck dumps up to a thousand board feet of oak at a time into a mechanical bin, which jiggles and shuffles boards to feed them, one at a time, onto a large conveyor. The conveyor then carries them past the trained eyes of the lumber grader, who sorts them by pulling boards into different piles. By the time one board makes it onto the conveyor, its nearest neighbors from the tree are long gone and far away. This is quite a different concept from the photos you may have seen of hardwood logs being sawn, stickered and placed back in the original order just as they were cut from the tree.

I've learned that the very best wood is the wood you've gotten yourself. For me, this means keeping my eyes on the forests and neighborhoods in my community, accepting gifts of trees when they are offered and planting new trees in thanks and appreciation. People have deep feelings for the trees in their yards and in most cases would prefer that a craftsman make use of them rather than have them go into the fireplace or dump. I have a friend, Bob, who has a portable sawmill and will cut logs into lumber for an hourly rate. I can keep and dry lumber in the order that it was cut—which has greater significance to me because it comes from my community and was a gift from friends. I can make sure that there is more of it coming and I can protect it for future generations.

If I were new to woodworking, I'd make friends with someone with one of these saws. I'd call one of the manufacturers and say, "I'm interested in one of your saws. Have you sold one to someone in my town? Where could I see one at work?" Chances are, you'll find someone just like my friend Bob. Of course, the drawback to this approach is that it takes so long. You have to air-dry wood outdoors for several months under cover, then move it indoors for about a year per inch of thickness. Heated and air-conditioned space is best.

Ideals are often complicated. They take time and effort. But it is good to have an objective in mind. In the meantime, I have found that often the most expensive woods are not the most beautiful, and that the characteristics which may make a board unsuitable for some uses, and therefore less costly, may make it more desirable to someone like myself.

INLAYING THE TOP

STEP 1
Cut Strips for the Top

After the dovetails are cut and fitted, cut strips of cherry to attach to the insides of the front, back and sides to broaden the area available for inlaying. Miter these just a little bit oversize in length, and use #0 size biscuits to attach them to the inside top edges of the box parts. Before gluing these parts in place, chamfer the bottom edge and sand the parts. This will be difficult once these pieces are glued in place. Be careful, when gluing them in place, that the ends extend just barely beyond the edges of the mitered dovetails. This will allow you to trim them off again with the dozuki after the inlay is in place.

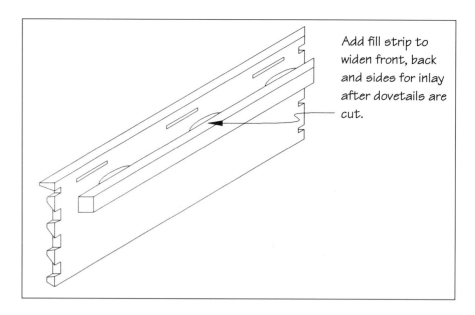

Add fill strip to widen front, back and sides for inlay after dovetails are cut.

STEP 2
Make the Inlay

To make the inlay, follow the procedure used for making the inlay for the tea chest in chapter twelve, except plane the sycamore to ½" in thickness and resaw the walnut banding to about ³⁄₃₂", so that the finished banding will be about ⅝" in dimension to better fit the proportions of this larger box. Before shaping and inlaying the top edge of the box, use the table saw to cut the top parts away from the bottom, unlike the technique used in making the tea chest, which was assembled before the top was cut away. This makes dadoing the top edge for the raised panel, shaping the top angle of the lid pieces and inlaying them easier operations. Unlike inlaying the tea chest, cut the angle in the top edge first, and then inlay it using the router table techniques described previously.

INSTALLING DRAWERS AND DIVIDERS

STEP 1
Cut Dadoes and Mortises in the Sides and Top

Before the box is assembled, perform several routing operations to provide for drawer guide strips in the sides, top compartment slide strips in the front and back, mortises for compartment dividers in the front and back, and a ³⁄₁₆" dado in the front, back and sides for the interior panel of the box. Use the ³⁄₁₆" carbide spiral end mill for all of these operations, changing the fence settings and arrangement of stop blocks as needed.

STEP 2
Make the Drawer and Trays

Make the bottom drawer using a mortise-and-tenon joint to connect the sides to the front and back, and use ⅛" Baltic birch for the drawer bottom. Fit the drawer sides to the drawer guides using the ³⁄₁₆" end mill in the router. Index the cut from the bottom edge of the drawer side so that the bottom edge of the drawer will be flush with the bottom edge of the box, and a tight fit can be adjusted

Use the router table with fence, stop blocks and ³⁄₁₆" carbide spiral cutter to route for the bottom, sliding tray guides and dividers to fit in the front and back pieces, and for the bottom and drawer guides to fit in the sides. Use the router table to route channels in the drawer sides to fit the drawer guides.

by trimming the top edge of the drawer. To make sure that the drawer moves freely on the guide, adjust the fence in slightly to widen the cut with a second pass. Make the trays using the mortise-and-tenon technique shown in chapter eight. The technique for making the dividers is shown in chapter twelve.

STEP 3
Cut the Drawer Opening
Before assembly, cut away the areas on the sides where the drawer will fit, and cut the chamfer to fit the shape of the drawer. Trim the bottom panel to fit into the ³⁄₁₆″ dado, and sand all the inside surfaces of the box.

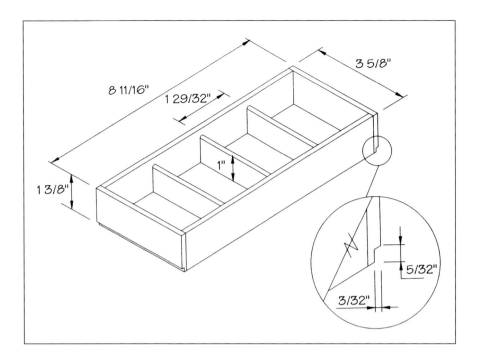

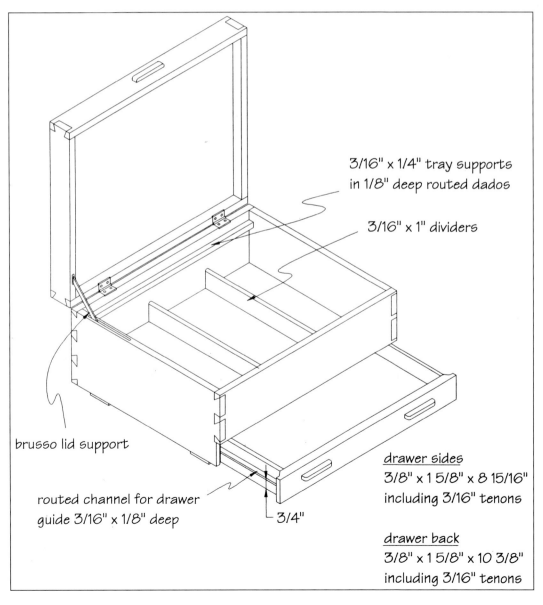

3/16" x 1/4" tray supports
in 1/8" deep routed dados

3/16" x 1" dividers

brusso lid support

routed channel for drawer
guide 3/16" x 1/8" deep

3/4"

drawer sides
3/8" x 1 5/8" x 8 15/16"
including 3/16" tenons

drawer back
3/8" x 1 5/8" x 10 3/8"
including 3/16" tenons

ASSEMBLE THE BOX

STEP 1
Glue Up the Sides

Next, put the front and back together around the interior dividers, spread glue on the pins and tails and push the sides into place. Use bar clamps to pull the sides in tight, checking with a tape measure to make sure the box is square.

STEP 2
Assemble the Top

Before assembling the top, put it together for a trial assembly and use the dozuki to recut the corners, trimming the inlaid corners to match. As before, spread the joint out just a bit, the width of a saw kerf, and cut down into the joint, being careful not to cut into the dovetail. Rather than overcut, you can stop short of cutting too far, pull the joint back apart and finish the cut with a straight chisel. Make the raised panel top using the same techniques used to make the top for the tea chest, and sand it on the inside before assembly. Cut the dado for the panel to fit in the top with the table saw and a ¼" dado blade. Position the cut so that the angled surfaces of the top panel will meet the angled edge of the dovetailed frame. In assembling the top, put a bit of glue in the dado at the center of the sides of the top to keep the panel centered in the frame, while leaving it free to expand and contract as needed, and apply glue to the pins and dovetails as in assembling the base. To check the square of the lid, place it on the base and feel to see that it lines up flush on all sides.

After inlaying is complete, use the dozuki saw again to cut into the miter with the joint open just a bit. It is good to make sure that the frame is square as you do this to get a good fit.

Assemble the box with glue spread on the pins and tails.

FINISHING THE BOX

To complete the jewelry box, sand the outside, chamfer the edges very slightly where the top meets the bottom, and chamfer the bottom edges of the box and the drawer front. Assemble the drawer and, after the sliding compartments are made, make a rabbet cut on each end so that it will fit down over the guides and slide smoothly without touching either the inside of the box or the sliding-tray ends. Make little walnut feet, tenoned to fit in mortises routed in the bottom of the box after assembly, to lift it slightly above the table and walnut pulls as described previously.

Use drawn brass hinges, which you can install using the same technique described in making the tea chest, and a lid support from Woodcraft Supply on this project. Use the plunge router to route the mortise for the lid support, and a ¼″ brad-point drill bit to drill in the top for the other end to fit.

To assemble the top, spread glue on the pins and tail and just a small dab only at the center of the dado where the panel fits. This is to keep the panel centered in the lid during changes in humidity.

CHAPTER 14

Rachel's Jewelry Cabinet

This jewelry cabinet is based on a design from about 1978. A woman had seen my inlaid boxes in a gallery in Dallas and contacted me to make a jewelry cabinet for her daughter Rachel, who was just becoming a teenager. The first cabinet was made of quilted maple and had hangers for necklaces on the doors and at the back, as well as two drawers in the bottom. It is impossible for me to go back to old projects without adding what I've learned in the intervening years. This cabinet is based on photographs from my files with some new features added to make it more useful than the original design. The folding fabric wings provide a convenient way to hang necklaces, pins and, with the open-weave cloth used, earrings of either the hook or post type. The cabinet is made with exposed mortise-and-tenon joints that are locked in place with walnut wedges. The doors are of frame and panel construction, with mortise-and-tenon joints as well. The simple inlaid bands of walnut highlight the design without attempting to overpower the highly figured maple. The front door panels are resawn and book-matched. Visual weight is important to consider in the design of a freestanding cabinet. The broader stance given by the feet makes one feel more secure in opening the doors. I reduced the size of the top, cutting it shorter on both ends and across the front after milling it to fit the sides, to keep the cabinet from feeling top heavy and, in selecting wood for the side panels, I oriented the pattern of the grain to move from the bottom front corner to the top rear. This visual weight helps to add a sense of security to the feel of the cabinet when the doors are open. These small details in the selection and arrangement of the material add a great deal to the finished work.

SELECTION OF MATERIAL

I purchased the material used in this cabinet at the same lumber dealer I had gotten material from for the first version eighteen years ago, Nations Hardwoods in Prairie Grove, Arkansas. This dealer sells only air-dried lumber, most of which was cut and dried back when I was starting out as a woodworker. While it is stored in relatively dry conditions, the building is not heated or air conditioned, so I plan for some shrinkage from changing moisture conditions in its use.

MATERIALS LIST

Top and bottom	2 pcs.	$\frac{3}{4}'' \times 6\frac{7}{8}'' \times 16\frac{1}{4}''^1$
Sides	2 pcs.	$\frac{3}{4}'' \times 5\frac{1}{2}'' \times 21\frac{3}{8}''$
Middle shelf	1 pc.	$\frac{3}{4}'' \times 5\frac{1}{4}'' \times 14''$
Feet	2 pcs.	$\frac{7}{8}'' \times 2\frac{3}{8}'' \times 7\frac{1}{8}''$
Drawer guides	6 pcs.	$\frac{1}{2}'' \times \frac{3}{8}'' \times 5\frac{1}{8}''$
Walnut wedges	8 pcs.	$\frac{3}{8}'' \times 1'' \times \frac{1}{16}''$ (tapering to $\frac{1}{32}''$ thick)
Walnut inlay strips	4 pcs.	$\frac{1}{8}'' \times \frac{1}{8}'' \times 26''$
Doors		
Outside stiles	2 pcs.	$\frac{3}{4}'' \times 1\frac{1}{4}'' \times 20\frac{1}{8}''$
Inside stiles	2 pcs.	$\frac{3}{4}'' \times 1'' \times 20\frac{1}{8}''$
Upper rails	2 pcs.	$\frac{3}{4}'' \times 1\frac{1}{4}'' \times 6\frac{11}{16}''^2$
Lower rails	2 pcs.	$\frac{3}{4}'' \times 1\frac{1}{2}'' \times 6\frac{11}{16}''^2$
Pulls	2 pcs.	$\frac{3}{8}'' \times 1\frac{5}{8}'' \times \frac{5}{8}''^3$
Interior wing supports		
Vertical parts	8 pcs.	$\frac{5}{8}'' \times \frac{3}{4}'' \times 13\frac{5}{16}''$
Arms	2 pcs.	$\frac{5}{16}'' \times 1'' \times 6\frac{5}{16}''^4$
	2 pcs.	$\frac{5}{16}'' \times 1'' \times 5\frac{7}{16}''^4$
	2 pcs.	$\frac{5}{16}'' \times 1'' \times 4\frac{9}{16}''^4$
	2 pcs.	$\frac{5}{16}'' \times 1'' \times 3\frac{11}{16}''^4$
Drawers		
Bottoms	3 pcs.	$4\frac{1}{2}'' \times 12\frac{13}{16}''$
Dividers	3 pcs.	$\frac{1}{8}'' \times 1\frac{1}{8}'' \times 4\frac{1}{2}''$ (for top drawer)
Pulls	6 pcs.	$\frac{1}{4}'' \times \frac{1}{4}'' \times 1\frac{7}{8}''$

Top drawers		
Front	1 pc.	$\frac{5}{8}'' \times 1\frac{1}{2}'' \times 13\frac{7}{16}''^5$
Sides	2 pcs.	$\frac{3}{8}'' \times 1\frac{1}{2}'' \times 5\frac{5}{16}''$
Back	1 pc.	$\frac{3}{8}'' \times 1\frac{1}{2}'' \times 13\frac{7}{16}''$
Middle drawer		
Front	1 pc.	$\frac{5}{8}'' \times 1\frac{3}{4}'' \times 13\frac{7}{16}''^5$
Sides	2 pcs.	$\frac{3}{8}'' \times 1\frac{3}{4}'' \times 5\frac{5}{16}''$
Back	1 pc.	$\frac{3}{8}'' \times 1\frac{3}{4}'' \times 13\frac{7}{16}''$
Bottom drawer		
Front	1 pc.	$\frac{5}{8}'' \times 2\frac{1}{2}'' \times 13\frac{7}{16}''^5$
Sides	2 pcs.	$\frac{3}{8}'' \times 2\frac{1}{2}'' \times 5\frac{5}{16}''$
Back	1 pc.	$\frac{3}{8}'' \times 2\frac{1}{2}'' \times 13\frac{7}{16}''$
Hardware		
Brusso knife hinges	2 pr.	$\frac{5}{16}''$
Bullet catches	2 pcs.	$\frac{1}{4}''$ (with catch cups)
Brass pins	16 pcs.	$\frac{3}{16}'' \times \frac{3}{4}''$ (for pivoting wings)
	27 pcs.	$\frac{1}{8}'' \times \frac{5}{8}''$ (for necklaces)

[1] After mortising, cut to $6\frac{3}{4}'' \times 16''$
[2] Measurement includes $\frac{3}{4}''$ tenon at each end.
[3] Measurement includes $\frac{3}{16}''$ tenon length.
[4] Measurement includes $\frac{1}{2}''$ tenon length.
[5] Size of original piece to cut coves.

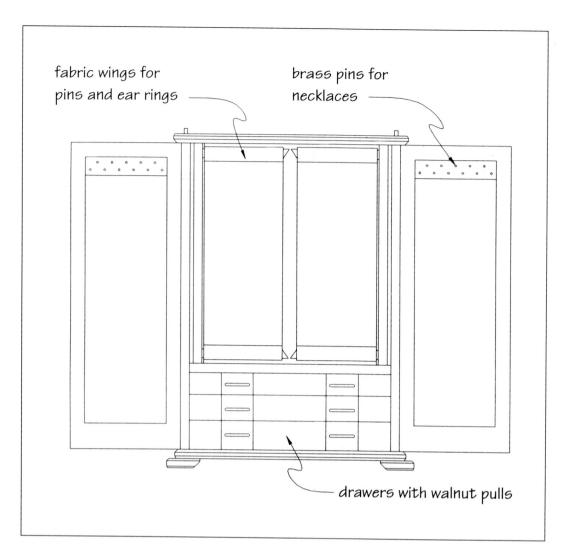

fabric wings for pins and ear rings

brass pins for necklaces

drawers with walnut pulls

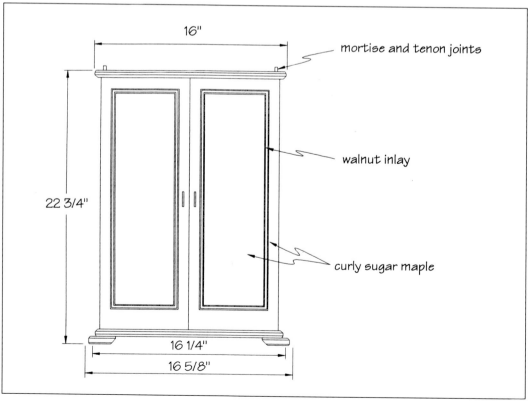

16"

mortise and tenon joints

walnut inlay

22 3/4"

curly sugar maple

16 1/4"

16 5/8"

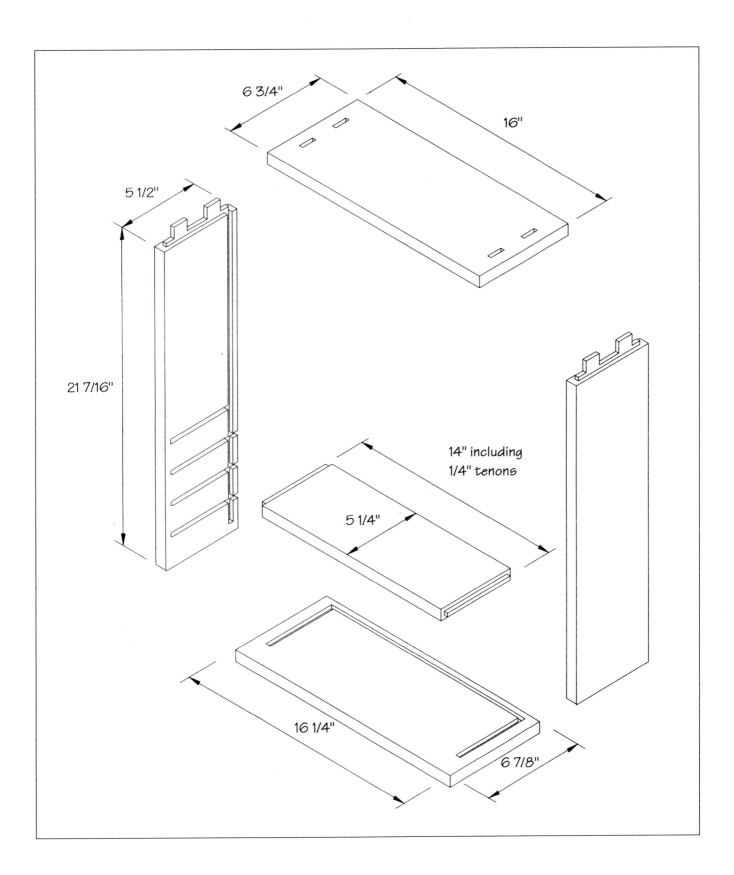

6 3/4"

16"

5 1/2"

21 7/16"

14" including
1/4" tenons

5 1/4"

16 1/4"

6 7/8"

PREPARING MATERIALS

I follow a practice of cutting my lumber into rough parts before planing to final dimensions. This allows me to straighten any warped or twisted boards on the jointer before planing. It also gives me more control with the planer when surfacing figured woods. Often, the orientation of the grain will change over the length of an 8′ board; the effectiveness of the planer at achieving a perfect surface will also change. I am also very selective and careful when cutting to ensure that the most heavily figured woods and pleasing grain patterns are reserved for use in the door panels, stiles and rails which are the most visible parts of the project.

MAKING THE CHEST

STEP 1
Route the Mortises
Use a plunge router with a ⅜″ spiral cutter to route the mortises in the top and bottom. The mortises in the bottom are only ¼″ deep, and are only used to position the sides in place while screws are used to secure the bottom to the sides. The top, however, uses no screws and requires a two-step mortising process. Use screws to secure the bottom to the sides because this technique allows you to take the cabinet apart with little difficulty in the event that repairs are ever needed, and also avoids having tenons in the way of attaching the feet. Route the through mortises in the top first, and then adjust the depth of the plunge router to cut the shallower mortises in the top and bottom.

STEP 2
Square the Mortises
After routing the mortises in the top, chisel the corners of the mortises square to fit the square corners of the tenons.

Clamp the cabinet top to the workbench, using a setup block to hold stop blocks the right distance apart to form the mortise. The setup block length is determined by measuring the router base width, adding the length of the mortise and subtracting the width of the router bit.

Turn the top piece over and change the router depth to route the inside of the top and bottom for the non-invisible part of the tenon to fit. Route the bottom in the same manner.

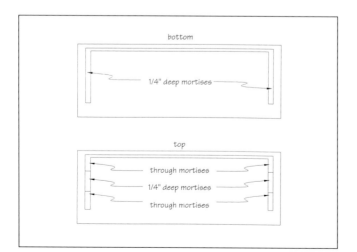

bottom

1/4" deep mortises

top

through mortises

1/4" deep mortises

through mortises

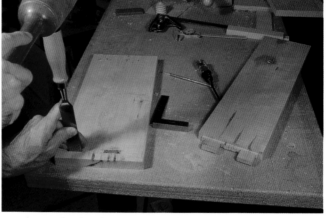

Use a straight chisel to square up the mortises to fit the tenons.

STEP 3

Cut the Tenons

Cut the tenons on the table saw with a shop-made tenoning jig that follows the ripping fence. This has become a very common shop item for most woodworkers, modeled after cast-iron manufactured jigs. (The steps in making a tenon are shown in the photos at right.) The twin tenons for attaching the sides to the top require additional steps. Cut the shape of the tenons conventionally using the tenoning jig—but removing the stock from between the tenons is a job for the band saw, as shown below. Then use the band saw to cut the slots for wedges to fit into the tenons. To do this, use the accessory fence on the band saw, and clamp a block of wood to the fence to limit the length of cut. Cut into the tenon, back the workpiece out, turn the cabinet side over to cut the other tenon and then adjust the fence to make second cuts in each tenon. Cut the short tenons on the sides, and the ends of the midshelf between the drawers and the upper section, using the techniques used for the longer tenons, adjusting the height of cut on the saw to allow for their length.

STEP 4

Route the Mortises for the Shelf

Use the plunge router to cut the dadoes in the sides for the midshelf to fit. Clamp both sides together and route them at the same time, routing in from both sides and leaving a ¾″ space in the middle between the sides so that the dado will be hidden from the front of the cabinet.

STEP 5

Route Dovetails in the Sides for the Drawer Guides

To fit the drawer guides in the sides, route dovetailed channels that enter from the back of the cabinet and are blind at the front, stopping about ⅝″ short to avoid

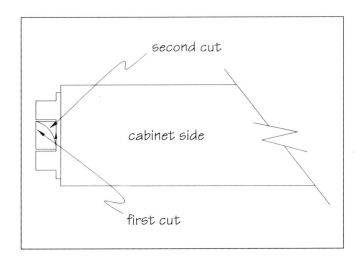

Use a shop-made tenoning jig on the table saw to begin shaping the tenons. Make both cuts with the face of the side against the jig.

Use the cutoff box on the table saw to complete the cuts forming the tenons on the cabinet sides. A stop block clamped to the cutoff box accurately positions the cut.

Use the plunge router to cut the dado for the midshelf to fit. By clamping and routing both sides at the same time, you can be certain the shelf will fit level between the two sides. Route in from both sides, leaving space at the middle to hide the dado at the front of the cabinet sides.

interfering with the drawer fronts. Carefully mark out the locations in pencil, and plan the guides to run at the center of each drawer. Use a guide piece clamped to the drawer sides to control the position of the router, with the sides held firmly together; routing both sides in the same operation, you can be certain that the drawer guides will come out at the same height.

STEP 6
Make the Drawer Guides
To make the drawer guides, use the router and a dovetail bit as shown in the drawing below. Prepare the stock in long strips and cut the pieces to length after they have been fitted to the dovetail slots in the cabinet sides. Use the sanding disk to round the front edges to fit into the round ends of the slots, trim the inside edges down to slide freely within a ¼″ slot, and make a saw cut on the opposite end to allow for the ⅛″ Baltic birch back panel.

Use the router to form the dovetail slots for the drawer guides. Because of the hardness of the sugar maple, first route each slot with a ¼″ straight-cut bit, and then set up for a finish cut with a 14° dovetail bit.

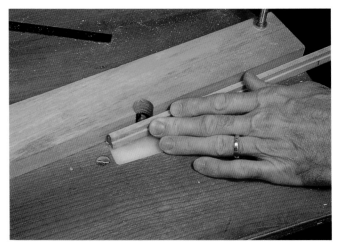

Using the dovetail bit, route the drawer guide stock to fit the slots in the cabinet sides.

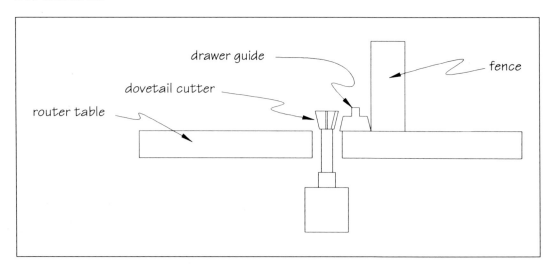

STEP 7
Resaw the Door Panels

Begin making the doors by resawing the door panels. Pass one side of the stock across the jointer if it is not already perfectly flat. Then set up the fence on the band saw so that the blade cuts right down the center of the panel stock. Band saw blades tend to track one way or the other, so it's a good idea to check the particular blade with a test piece to be certain that the angle of the fence is correct before cutting the figured stock. Pay close attention to the movement and pattern of the grain in selecting material for the stiles and rails of the doors. I like for the center stiles to be cut from a single piece of wood if possible, and I like to take special care in arranging the parts so that the left and right doors mirror each other, giving symmetry to the finished piece.

STEP 8
Cut the Door Rails and Stiles

Start by cutting the door stiles to the exact size, width and length. The door rails will need to be tenoned to fit the mortises in the stiles, so cut them 1½″ oversize in length to allow for ¾″-long tenons on each end.

STEP 9
Cut the Mortises in the Stiles

As in all mortising and tenoning operations, start by cutting the mortises: This will allow you to get an exact fit.

Use a shop-made jig with the plunge router and a ⅜″ spiral plunge cutter to route the mortises. To use this jig, clamp the workpiece in place and operate the router back and forth between the stops, plunging deeper with each

Use the band saw with the fence and stop block to cut the slots in the tenons for the walnut edges to fit.

Arrange the cabinet door panels and stiles as they will be used in the doors, and mark them in pencil to indicate their location.

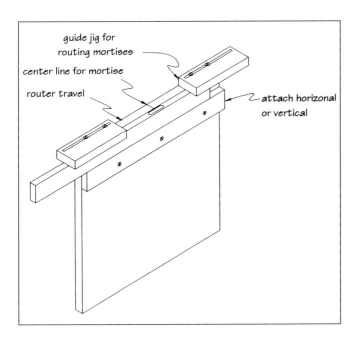

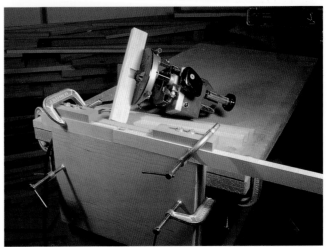

Use a shop-made jig with the plunge router and fence to mortise the door stiles for the rails to fit. Place the stock in the jig with the face side out, so it is in contact with the router fence, to control the position of the cut.

Adjust the postion of the guide block for the final cut, with the face side still against the guide block. Cut a test piece first to check the fit of the tenon in the routed mortises.

Use a few quick strokes with the rasp to shape the tenon to fit the mortise, and clean up in the corners with a straight chisel.

Use a ⅛″ slotting cutter in the router table to cut the dadoes for the panels to fit. The height of the cut is set to bring the panels flush with the stiles and rails on the front of the cabinet.

cut, until the router depth stop is reached. By using a stop block clamped to the side of the jig opposite the work-piece, only one measurement needs be made. In order to get the best possible fit, index all the pieces from the same side. Route both top left-hand door stiles, and then reverse the setup to route the top right. Because the bottom rails of the cabinet are larger, simplify the tenoning by making the lower mortises longer. This requires more mortising setups to route the bottom door-stile mortises and adjusting the width of travel between the stops on the jig.

STEP 10
Tenon the Door Rails
Once the mortises are cut, you have a point of reference for cutting the tenons on the upper and lower door rails. Tenon a test piece to make certain of the fit in the mortise before making all the cuts on the workpieces. In cutting the door tenons, follow nearly the same sequence described for making the cabinet sides.

STEP 11
Fitting the Tenons and Door Panels
To round the shoulders of the tenons to fit the mortises, speed things up by cutting away part of the corners with the band saw, and then finish up the shaping of the tenons with a rasp and a straight chisel.

In order for the panels to fit in the door frames, route dadoes in the stiles and rails using the router and a ⅛″ slotting cutter. Set up the fence to limit the cut to ¼″ deep, and set the router height so that the panel will be flush with the face side of the door frame.

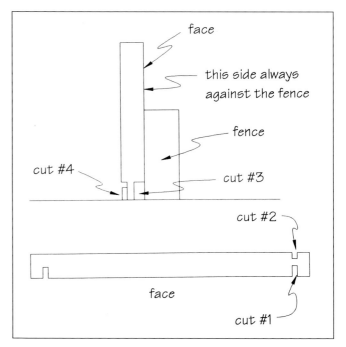

STEP 12

Fit the Door Panels

When the door frames are complete, assemble one and take the exact measurements of the inside space. Cut the panel to a dimension $7/16''$ oversize in width and $15/32''$ oversize in length. This is to give material to make the $1/4'' \times 3/16''$ tongue around the perimeter to hold the panel in the frame. Leave about $1/16''$ in a panel this size to allow for expansion in wet weather, but it should not expand in length, so leave only about $1/32''$ in length to ease assembly. Before cutting the tongue on the panels, route a test piece to make certain it fits the dadoes routed in the stiles and rails.

STEP 13

Assemble the Doors

Before assembling the door parts around the panels, assemble them without glue and route the inside edges where the door frames will intersect the panels with a 45° chamfering bit. Then use a straight chisel to finish the cut, following the chamfered edge into the corners. While the doors are assembled, use a sanding block to sand the chamfered edges. Use a V-groove bit in the router to route a matching chamfer on the door panels, and use a sanding block to smooth the routed cut.

To do the final assembly of the doors, squeeze glue in the mortises and use a $1/4''$ dowel to spread the glue around evenly. Position the top and bottom rails into one side, push the panel into position and then position the opposite door stile. Clamp the assembled door with bar clamps and check it for square by measuring corner to corner on the diagonal. If the door is square, both corner-to-corner measurements will be exactly the same. If the door is out of square, release the clamps and, standing the door up on one of its long corners, try to move it into square. When both diagonal measurements are the same, re-clamp the door, checking it one more time to make sure that the door has remained square in the re-clamping process.

STEP 14

Inlay the Doors

Inlaying the doors of Rachel's cabinet is a very easy process. Use a plunge router with a fence and a $1/8''$ straight-cut router bit. Start by marking the starting and stopping points of the router's travel on the assembled door. Arrange these points to minimize the amount of cleanup that must be done with the chisel. Because the outer stiles and top rails are the same size, they require one router setting; the bottom rail, being wider, requires that the router fence be moved for a second setup, and the center stiles require

Clamp safety blocking on the router table to protect your fingers from being pulled into the cutter.

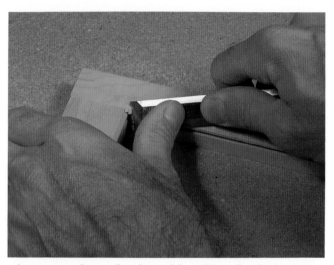

After routing the inside edges of the stiles and rails, finish out the chamfer, cutting into the corners with a straight chisel. Hold the chisel flat against the existing chamfer and use it to guide the cuts from both directions into the corner.

With pencil, ruler and square, lay out the corners of the inlay design, indicating the starting and stopping points for routing the inlay channels.

a third. Moving the router from left to right keeps the router bit pulling the router fence toward the door. A ⅛" solid carbide spiral-end mill works great for this job, giving a smooth, even cut. Use a straight chisel to lengthen the router cuts so that they intersect, and use a ⅛" straight chisel to make sure the bottom of the routed channel is clean and flat.

Prepare the inlay stock by passing a piece of walnut through the jointer, making sure it is square. Then set up the fence on the table saw and rip the walnut stock to pieces about ¹⁄₁₆" thicker than the needed inlay. Use a tapered sanding disk to sand the walnut stock to the finished thickness. Check the thickness of the inlay stock by at-

tempting to slip one edge of it into the routed channel, and measure with the dial caliper to be certain that the stock is an even thickness on both sides. If it is not, the angle of the sanding disk must be changed. Use the table saw and a zero-clearance insert to cut the finished inlay stock into thin strips of inlay material. Miter the ends to the right length using a straight chisel, and glue the strips in place, using C-clamps and strips of wood to bear down evenly on the inlay strips and to protect the back sides of the doors from being marred by the clamps. When the glue has had a chance to dry, sand the inlay strips flush to the surrounding surface.

Use a straight chisel to square and finish the routed channels.

Use the tapered sanding disk in the table saw to size the inlay stock to fit the routed space. Push the stock between the sanding disk and fence, and finish by pulling the stock from the other side. Flexing the strip helps to keep it tight against the fence. This is not an operation to perform with a regular blade in the table saw.

Miter the ends of the strips and cut them to length with a straight chisel, fitting one end and then the other around the doors.

Use the table saw with an auxillary fence clamped on the top to cut the coves in the drawer fronts. Cut all three drawers at the same time to provide a surface large enough to follow the fence safely. Raise the height of the saw in very small increments, forming the coves through very shallow cuts.

STEP 15
Make the Drawers

A special feature of the drawers is the recessed pulls, which allow the doors to close over them. Make the drawer facings of ⅝″ stock to allow for the cove-cut areas for the pulls, but make the sides and back from ⅜″ stock. The thinner stock can be resawn from 1″ material, giving twice as much wood for the money, but also providing plenty of strength for a drawer of this size. Use the table saw to form the coves on the drawer fronts. This is done with an auxiliary fence clamped at an angle on the table saw. This must be done with gradual increases in blade height and making a series of cuts, so cut all three drawer faces as a unit, cutting them to size after the cove cut and sanding are complete.

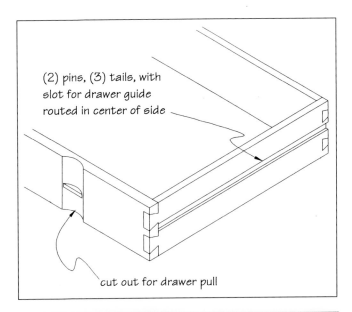

(2) pins, (3) tails, with slot for drawer guide routed in center of side

cut out for drawer pull

Use a marking gauge to lay out the thickness of the drawer sides on the drawer fronts. This is your first step in designing the dovetail layout.

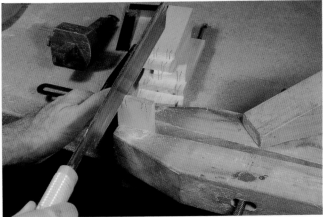

Cut the dovetails with a dozuki saw. The dovetails on the front of the drawers are laid out to decrease in size from the largest drawer to the smallest to stay in proportion, while the pins and tails at the back of the drawers are designed to allow for the positions of the drawer guides.

Use a small chisel and mallet to finish the dovetails.

Use a knife to scribe the dovetails on the ends of the drawer fronts and backs to cut the pins.

STEP 16
Cut the Drawer Dovetails

In laying out the dovetails on the drawers, use a sliding T-bevel, a steel rule, a square, a pencil, a marking gauge and a small knife. Arrange the dovetails to increase in size proportionately to the size of the drawer on the fronts, and also to allow for the drawer guide slots in the centers of the sides. First cut the tails with a Japanese dozuki saw, and use a chisel and mallet to remove the waste between the tails. Make the job a bit easier by making a table saw cut to remove a bit of the waste. Keep the blade low enough that there is still a little bit to chisel, rather than cut too high and make an awful mark. Use a small carving knife to scribe the dovetails on the ends of the front and back pieces for cutting the pins, and complete the markings with the small square and a marking gauge. Cut the pins using the dozuki and a straight chisel.

STEP 17
Cut the Drawer Sides

To cut the drawer sides to fit the drawer guides, use a router and a ¼″ straight-cut bit. I've found it best to route a test piece and check its fit in the trial-assembled cabinet before ruining a drawer side with carefully cut dovetails.

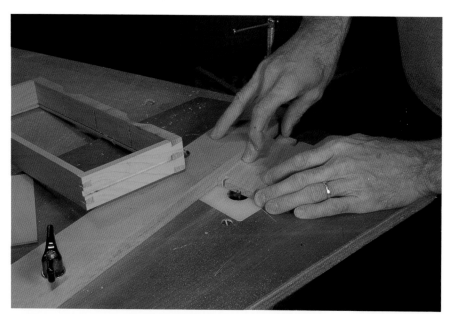

Use the router table and a ¼″ straight-cut bit to route the drawer sides to fit the drawer guides after the cabinet has been trial-assembled. It is a good idea to route test pieces and check their fit in the cabinet before actually cutting the carefully dovetailed drawer sides.

Check the fit and operation of the drawer sides before assembling the drawers.

Use the plunge router and fence to mortise for the knife hinges, then square the cut with a straight chisel to fit the hinges. Note the holes drilled for the earring and pin hangers.

Make the drawer bottoms from ⅛" Baltic birch plywood, and use a ⅛" straight-cut router bit to cut the slot for it to fit. Route for dividers to fit in the top drawer using a ⅛" straight-cut router bit and following the procedure used to form the dividers for the tea chest (chapter twelve).

STEP 18
Assemble the Drawer
Use a squeeze bottle to apply glue to all the surfaces of the pins and tails as you assemble the drawers, and spread the glue evenly on the surfaces with a thin stick. Then press the pieces together around the bottom and clamp as necessary. Check the drawer for square by measuring from corner to corner. If one measurement is longer than another, squeeze the drawer into square. Also, set the drawer down on a flat surface, like the top of the table saw, and check to see that it doesn't rock; this would also indicate the drawer is out of square.

STEP 19
Hinge the Doors
Knife hinges are easy to use, but the hinge mortises must be cut before the cabinet is assembled. Use the plunge router and fence with a ⁵⁄₁₆" straight-cut router bit. Set the depth of the cut on the router to equal the thickness of one blade of the knife hinge, and use the bearing plate between the blades to determine the door clearance at the top and bottom. After fitting the knife to the top and bottom, trial-assemble the cabinet and use a pencil to transfer the markings for the inside corners of the hinges to the doors, while they are held in position on the front of the cabinet. In laying out to the position of the hinges, leave a small clearance between the doors and the cabinet sides.

STEP 20
Install the Door Catches
Use ¼" bullet-type catches to secure the doors in the closed position. To install these, drill two holes, ¹⁷⁄₆₄" in diameter, in the base of the cabinet. To locate the position for these holes, fit the two sides into the base and use a straightedge to mark between the front edges of the sides: This will give you the closed position of the doors. After removing the sides, use the catch cups, positioning them along the line so that the edge of the catch cup that aligns with the door edge also aligns with the line marking the closed position of the doors. At the center of the catch cup is a hole used for tacking the catch cup in place on the door bottom. This hole is also the center point for the bullet, and by marking it with a tack, the position to drill the ⅜" hole can be accurately determined. Next drill the

With the doors held in position, and from the back of the cabinet, transfer the markings for the knife hinges to the back of the doors. This gives the stopping points for routing the hinge mortises in the doors.

With the door clamped firmly in the vertical position, route for the knife hinges to fit. Index the cut from the back edge of the door; use a straight chisel to square up the cut to fit the hinge.

holes in the bottom of the doors for the catch cups to fit. I use my Shop Smith set up for horizontal boring to complete this task. Drill just deep enough to position the raised surface of the cup flush with the door bottom when it is nailed in place.

STEP 21
Make and Install the Door Pulls
Use black walnut pulls, which are formed through a several-step process, on the cabinet doors. Use the plunge router to cut ⅛″ mortises in the door fronts to a depth just over the length of the tenons on the pulls.

STEP 22
Make the Drawer Pulls
Route a mortise across the cove cuts in the drawer facings with a ¼″ straight-cut bit in the plunge router. Carefully mark the start and stop points on the inside of the cove with a pencil. Cutting the mortise before making the pulls allows you to check the exact fit of the stock before the pulls are cut to length and shaped. To make the pulls, cut the walnut stock to the length of the mortises cut in the drawer fronts and, with the pieces taped together, use the ⅛″ roundover bit in the router to shape the ends to fit the mortises. Then route the pulls with a 45° chamfering bit, doing the ends first and the sides last, and treating these as separate operations to keep your fingers well away from the bit. To route the back side of the pulls—you want to route only the portion not enclosed by the mortise—set up stop blocks on the router table to control the length of cut.

STEP 23
Make the Wings
The folding wings that hold pins and earrings are made with mortise-and-tenon joints, and have brass pins and washers for pivoting. Use the same techniques outlined for making the doors. I bore the holes for the hinge pins using a ³⁄₁₆″ bit that I cut to half its normal length and reground for drilling wood. Longer drill bits will tend to bend and follow the wood grain; this is reduced with a shorter bit. Position the drill to bore right at the center of each end of the vertical pieces. To drill the matching holes in the top and the midshelf, make a template of scrap wood, with the holes for the hinge pins marked on it. Drill through it in the positions marked for the centerlines of the pins and, with a nail, use this template to mark the inside of the top of the cabinet. Align the center of the template with the center line of the top. To mark the midshelf, use the same technique, but turn the template

Using the drill press, drill holes in the bottom of the cabinet for the bullet catches to fit. To accurately position the holes, lay a straightedge between the sides of the trial-assembled cabinet and trace a line along its edge. Then measure from the front edge of the catch plate to the nail hole at its center. This process gives the distance to mark out from the line for the bullet catch to fit.

Use the plunge router and fence to route for the door pulls, cutting about ¹⁄₆₄″ deeper than the length of the tenons on the pulls.

over, marking through from the opposite side. Use the ³⁄₁₆″ drill bit in the drill press to drill for the pins to fit. To make the pins, use the same technique used for cutting the brass hinge pins for the boxes in chapters nine and ten.

STEP 24
Install the Hangers
Use a ⅛″ brass rod, cut to length and with the ends polished, as hangers for jewelry on the insides of the doors

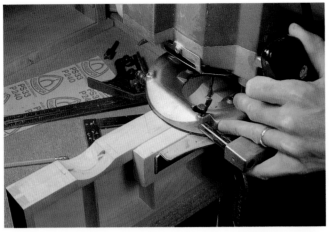

Use the plunge router to route mortises for the drawer pulls to fit in the coves on the drawer fronts.

Use a chamfering bit in the router to shape the drawer pulls. Route the ends, then the fronts and, with stop blocks in place to limit the cut to the open space behind the pulls, finish by routing the backs.

and the back of the cabinet. Cut the brass rod using the technique described for making the hinge pins. Then polish the ends by rolling the rods against a worn-out belt on the sander with your fingers, and then by buffing them on a polishing wheel with jeweler's rouge. Drill ⅛″ angled holes in thin maple stock to glue to the insides of the doors and the back panel to receive the pins, and lightly tack them in place when the cabinet is almost complete.

STEP 25
Install the Back Panel
Make the back panel from ⅛″-thick birch plywood, and glue the necklace hanging strip in place before final assembly of the cabinet.

The earring and pin hangers are assembled with mortise-and-tenon joints. Brass pins in the ends allow them to pivot in the cabinet.

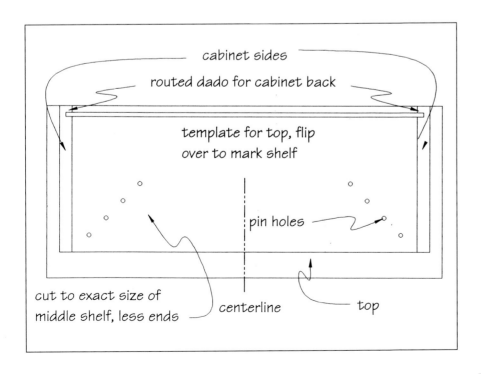

cabinet sides

routed dado for cabinet back

template for top, flip over to mark shelf

pin holes

cut to exact size of middle shelf, less ends

centerline

top

During assembly, first fit the hangers in the holes in the midshelf, then, after the top is slipped onto the tenons, turn the cabinet on its side and slip the pins in the top holes before pushing the top firmly in place.

Spread glue on both sides of the wedge and put a little in the saw kerf before tapping the wedge into place. The wedges expand the tenon to lock it in the mortise.

STEP 26
Sanding
Sand all the parts of the cabinet prior to finishing and assembly.

STEP 27
Finishing the Cabinet
Because of the complexity of the inside of the cabinet with its folding wings, do all the finishing prior to assembly. Apply a Danish oil finish to all parts of the cabinet, the doors and the drawers.

STEP 28
Final Assembly
Position the sides around the back panels and the midshelf with drawer guides in place, and then put the bottom on. With the cabinet standing up, slip the wing units into the holes in the midshelf and start the side tenons into the mortises in the top piece. Then, with the cabinet turned on its side, slide the wing units so that the brass pins start into the holes in the top, and push the top firmly into place. After turning the cabinet right side up, squeeze a little glue into the slots for the wedges and wipe a little glue on both sides of the wedges, and tap them into place. Use the dozuki to trim off the excess wedge material at the top of the tenons, sand the tenons flat and gently chamfer the ends of the tenons with a sanding block.

STEP 29
Making the Wedges

Make the wedges about ¼″ longer than needed to allow some to be trimmed off after being tapped into place. Make them by cutting stock to the thickness of the tenons and the length of the finished wedge. Use the miter guide on the table saw to adjust the angle so that the wedge tapers from just under the width of the band saw kerf to about ⅛″ thick. Turn the workpiece over with each cut, forming the wedges.

STEP 30
Install the Feet

The feet are simple blocks of sugar maple routed to accentuate the contours of the bottom of the cabinet and mounted with screws. Cover the screw holes with felt pads. This technique allows the cabinet to be disassembled in the event that repairs ever become necessary.

Cut the wedges for the wedged tenons on the table saw. Turn the ⅜″ stock over with each cut so that a portion of the desired angle is taken from each side.

CHAPTER 15

The Earring and Pin Chest

Many times, the designs used in my work have evolved from other projects. A number of years ago I made a cabinet for a friend to give to his wife for keeping and displaying her collection of pins. The cabinet was a free-form design, with dinosaur heads and parts attached in a sliding dovetail track enabling them to be rearranged—like a puzzle. I used the fabric wings for the first time in that piece: They make an excellent way to display and store fine jewelry without it being bunched in drawers where they can be nicked and scratched, more *worn-out* than *worn out*. This cabinet is designed to hold countless pairs of earrings and pins; with the brass pins installed in the doors, necklaces can also be hung. The drawer at the base provides conventional storage for larger items.

MAKING THE CABINET

STEP 1
Prepare the Stock for the Doors
I start by resawing the door panels on the band saw, but because my band saw has only a 6″ depth of cut, I cut the panels in two sections, each just a little wider than needed to form the L-shaped panels. Plane these panels to ¼″ thick. Next, cut the frame parts to size and cut the stiles to length, but leave the rails long so that they can be cut for the mitered corner.

STEP 2
Cut Mortises and Dadoes for the Doors
Use the plunge router to cut the mortises in the stiles, and then cut the tenons on the rails. Next, use the ⅛″ slotting cutter to cut the dadoes for the door panels to fit, cutting from end to end on the rails but cutting only between the mortises on the stiles. Set the slotting cutter height so that the finished panels will be flush with the outside surface of the stiles and rails.

MATERIALS LIST

Ash		$^{13}/_{16}''$
Black walnut		$1'' \times 1'' \times 20''$ (for raised inlay)
Tops and bottoms	4 pcs.	$^{3}/_{4}'' \times 1^{5}/_{8}'' \times 11^{1}/_{8}''$
	4 pcs.	$^{3}/_{4}'' \times 1^{5}/_{8}'' \times 8^{1}/_{8}''$
Vertical stretchers	3 pcs.	$^{3}/_{4}'' \times 1^{3}/_{8}'' \times 12^{1}/_{16}''$
Back panel	1 pc.	$^{1}/_{8}'' \times 6^{1}/_{8}'' \times 12^{9}/_{16}''$
Base and drawer front	2 pcs.	$^{3}/_{4}'' \times 1^{15}/_{16}'' \times 11^{1}/_{8}''$
	2 pcs.	$^{3}/_{4}'' \times 1^{15}/_{16}'' \times 8^{1}/_{8}''$
Interior wing supports	7 pcs.	$^{5}/_{8}'' \times ^{3}/_{4}'' \times 11^{15}/_{16}''$
	8 pcs.	$^{5}/_{16}'' \times 1'' \times 4^{3}/_{16}''^1$
	4 pcs.	$^{5}/_{16}'' \times 1'' \times 3^{5}/_{16}''$
	2 pcs.	$^{5}/_{16}'' \times 1'' \times 4^{7}/_{8}''$

Door parts

Stiles	2 pcs.	$^{3}/_{4}'' \times 1^{1}/_{2}'' \times 12''$
	2 pcs.	$^{3}/_{4}'' \times 1^{1}/_{4}'' \times 12''$
Rails	2 pcs.	$^{3}/_{4}'' \times 1^{1}/_{2}'' \times 10^{1}/_{2}''^2$
	2 pcs.	$^{3}/_{4}'' \times 1^{3}/_{4}'' \times 10^{1}/_{2}''^2$
	2 pcs.	$^{3}/_{4}'' \times 1^{1}/_{2}'' \times 4^{1}/_{8}''^3$
	2 pcs.	$^{3}/_{4}'' \times 1^{1}/_{2}'' \times 6^{1}/_{4}''^3$
	2 pcs.	$^{3}/_{4}'' \times 1^{3}/_{4}'' \times 4^{1}/_{8}''^3$
	2 pcs.	$^{3}/_{4}'' \times 1^{3}/_{4}'' \times 6^{1}/_{4}''^3$

Panels	2 pcs.	$^{1}/_{4}'' \times 3^{17}/_{32}'' \times 9^{1}/_{4}''^4$
	2 pcs.	$^{1}/_{4}'' \times 5^{11}/_{16}'' \times 9^{1}/_{4}''^4$
Tabs	2 pcs.	$^{1}/_{4}'' \times 1^{1}/_{4}'' \times ^{5}/_{16}''$
Corner blocks	4 pcs.	$^{1}/_{4}'' \times 1^{1}/_{4}'' \times 1^{3}/_{4}''$

Drawer parts

Sides	2 pcs.	$^{5}/_{16}'' \times 1^{15}/_{16}'' \times 6^{7}/_{8}''$
Back	1 pc.	$^{5}/_{16}'' \times 1^{15}/_{16}'' \times 9^{3}/_{8}''$
Bottom	1 pc.	$^{1}/_{8}'' \times 6^{5}/_{8}'' \times 9^{1}/_{4}''^5$
Pulls	2 pcs.	$^{5}/_{16}'' \times 1^{1}/_{4}'' \times ^{9}/_{16}''^5$

Hardware

Brainerd hinges	2 pcs.	$^{5}/_{16}'' \times 1'' \times ^{13}/_{16}''$ (open, with magnetic catches and catch plates)
Brass pins	16 pcs.	$^{1}/_{8}'' \times ^{5}/_{8}''$ (for necklace hangers)
	14 pcs.	$^{3}/_{16}'' \times ^{3}/_{4}''$ (pivot pins for wings)

[1]Length includes $^{1}/_{2}''$ tenons.
[2]Measurement before cutting miter joints.
[3]Measurement after cutting miter joints. Length includes $^{3}/_{4}''$ tenons.
[4]Finished dimension before gluing miter joint.
[5]Length includes tenons.

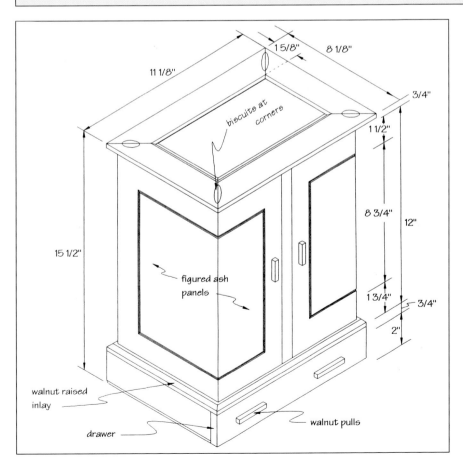

11 1/8"
1 5/8"
8 1/8"
3/4"
1 1/2"
biscuits at corners
8 3/4"
12"
1 3/4"
3/4"
2"
15 1/2"
figured ash panels
walnut raised inlay
drawer
walnut pulls

TOOLS LIST

Planer	Plunge router
Jointer	$^{3}/_{8}''$ and $^{1}/_{4}''$ carbide
Router table	spiral cutter
$^{1}/_{4}''$ straight-cut bit	45° chamfering bit
	$^{1}/_{8}''$ slotting cutter
Table saw	

Use the router table, ¼″ straight-cut bit, fence and stop blocks to cut slots for corner braces for the doors. Reposition the stop blocks to route the matching parts.

STEP 3
Cut the Door Panels to Size
Cut the panel parts to length and cut tongues on three sides, leaving the edges where the panel parts will be glued together alone. Use a V-groove bit to chamfer the panel edge where it will intersect the stiles and rails.

STEP 4
Dry-Assemble the Doors
Assemble the stiles and rails without glue so they can be pulled apart later, and use a 45° chamfering bit to chamfer the inside edges to match the panels. Use a straight chisel to cut into the corners, finishing the cut. (This is shown in detail in chapter fourteen.) Tilt the arbor of the saw to 45° to cut the rails to length, mitering them to fit back together to form the L-shaped doors, and while the saw is still at 45°, cut the miters in the panels, allowing just a little space for expansion in their width.

STEP 5
Make Corner Blocks
Use corner blocks to give strength to the corners of the doors, and use the router to route mortises to glue the blocks in place. In order for the corner blocks to fit, they must be five-sided, as shown at right center, and routed on the outside edges with a ⅛″ roundover bit to fit the mortises.

Use the miter cutoff box on the table saw to cut the five-sided corner blocks.

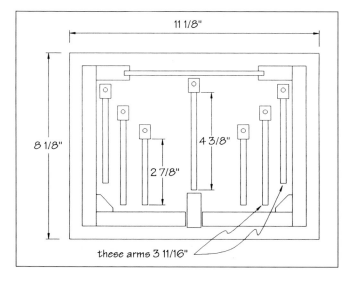

11 1/8"

8 1/8"

4 3/8"

2 7/8"

these arms 3 11/16"

STEP 6

Assemble the Doors

Assemble the rails with the corner blocks in place, using tape on the outside corners and tape pulled tight from tenon to tenon on the opposite side to pull the joint tight for gluing. Because you are gluing end grain, spread glue on both surfaces. Use the same technique to glue the panel parts together. To assemble the door units, first put the rails in place and then, with glue spread in the mortises, slide the stiles in place. Use bar clamps to pull the stiles tight to the rails while gluing.

STEP 7

Make the Top

Make the top and base using biscuit joints and #20 biscuits. Make a dado cut into the inside edges of the parts to hold the panel top and bottom in place. Before gluing the top, cut a chamfer on the panel and matching chamfer on the inside edges of the frame where they will be visible on the top; use a sanding block to sand these edges before assembly. When the top and bottom are assembled, use the plunge router to cut mortises for the vertical stretchers to fit. Use the fence on the plunge router to route the mortises that are parallel with the edge of the top and bottom frames, but use a clamped-in-place guide strip to route the mortises at 90° to the edge. Cut tenons on the ends to the vertical stretchers to fit the mortises, and plan these parts to be about 3⁄32″ longer than the doors to allow for clearance. Cut a 1⁄8″ dado on the inside edges of the back vertical stretchers for the back panel to fit and, using the plunge router, fence and a 1⁄8″ straight-cut router bit, cut the dadoes in the top and bottom pieces for the back panel to fit. Determine the setting for the fence by using a back vertical stretcher in place and measuring the distance to the 1⁄8″ dado. Use a piece of plywood with the pattern laid out on it for the center points of the brass pins for the pivoting wings, to mark the top and bottom pieces. Use a small drill bit to drill through the marked points, and then, with the template held firmly in place and with the corners lined up, mark the locations for the pins with nails. By turning the template over, you can mark the opposite part with the expectation that the marks will correspond despite any inaccuracies in their layout. Use the drill press and 3⁄16″ brad-point bit to drill the holes.

STEP 8

Make the Base

To make the base and drawer unit, use biscuit-joined corners and size the parts to equal the top and bottom, except for the portion cut away for the drawer to fit.

The L-shaped door panels fit into the upper and lower door rails before the stiles are glued in place.

Assemble the top and bottom panel sections with #20 biscuits. Spread glue in the biscuit slots and on the mitered surfaces.

With the plunge router and fence, cut the mortises for the vertical stretchers.

Use a jig with nails to locate the holes in the top section for the hinge pins for the fabric wings. Turn the piece over to locate the pin holes for the bottom panel. Then drill the holes using the drill press.

STEP 9

Make the Drawer

Before gluing the parts together, cut the ¼" dado for the drawer guide to fit, and cut a chamfer on the inside bottom edges of the parts. Use package sealing tape to pull the parts together tight, and check them for being square and flat, twisting them a bit or adjusting them before the glue sets. Make the drawer face and base parts from a continuous piece of ash so that the grain pattern and coloration will be continuous around the base unit. Make the drawer using the mortise-and-tenon technique used on other projects in this book. Use a ¼" straight-cut router bit to cut the drawer guide channels in the sides.

STEP 10

Make the Hanger Support Frame

In making the hanger support frame, mortise the vertical parts for the arms to fit, and then drill into the ends with a ³⁄₁₆" brad-point bit for the pins to fit. I use the Shop Smith as a horizontal borer for this operation, and use a stop block to control the location of the hole, with the fence clamped firmly in place at both ends to hold the workpiece.

STEP 11

Install the Raised Inlay

To prepare for the raised inlay, use the ⅛" slotting cutter in the router table, with only about ⅛" depth of cut. Center the height of the cut on the area remaining after the chamfered edges have been routed on the top and bottom pieces. To make the raised inlay, start with stock wide

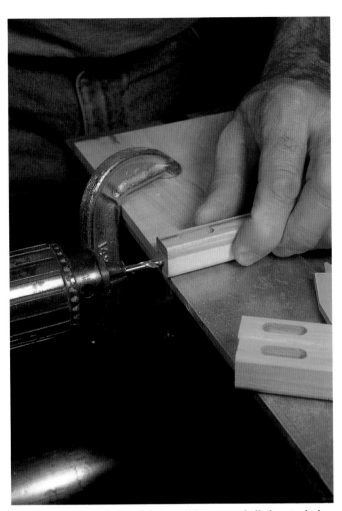

Use the Shop Smith as a horizontal borer to drill the pin holes in the vertical posts for the fabric wing assemblies. Note the mortises for attaching the arms.

Use a ⅛" slotting cutter in the router table to route for the raised inlay to fit.

enough to cut the tongue while still leaving a control surface, so that the piece will accurately follow the fence and surface of the router table. Use a ¼″ straight-cut router bit to cut in on both sides of the strip, leaving the ⅛″ tongue at the center. Use a dial caliper to check the thickness of the tongue, making sure it will fit into the slot around the base and top sections.

Use the 45° chamfering bit to route the profile on the raised strip. If the router bit has an unusually large space between the bearing and cutting surface, as some do, re-verse these steps and route the profile with the strip standing on edge. Use the table saw to cut the bearing surface of the strip away, and cut the depth of the tongue to fit into the slots. Use the cutoff box on the table saw to miter the raised inlay pieces and cut them to length.

Using a low plywood fence tacked in place allows you to safely hold the small stock. Spread glue in the slots, press the pieces in place and use tape to hold them while the glue sets.

Form the raised inlay by routing both sides of the strip with a ¼″ straight cutter, leaving a control surface on both sides of the cut. The center section remaining should be ⅛″ thick to fit exactly in the routed channel.

Form the profile of the raised inlay with a chamfering bit in the router table.

Set up the table saw to cut away the inlay strip to finished size, and then miter the strips to length with the cutoff box on the table saw.

STEP 12
Make the Pulls
Make the walnut pulls for the doors and drawer with techniques outlined previously, except use the 45° chamfering bit to shape the outside edges to match the chamfer used on the raised inlay. Use the router table with fence and a ⅛" straight-cut bit to mortise the doors and drawer for the pulls to fit, using stop blocks to position the cuts.

STEP 13
Install the Hardware
Route and chisel the mortises for hinges, drill for the magnetic catches and catch plates, and sand and finish all the parts prior to assembly.

STEP 14
Assemble the Chest
In assembly, put the back vertical stretchers in place along with the back panel and front vertical stretcher, and then place the hanger units and brass pins in the holes at the base. With glue in the mortises at the top, turn the unit on its side, slip the top onto the tenons and slide the top pins into their matching holes. Use bar clamps and cushions to pull the parts tight.

Use screws to attach the bottom to the vertical stretchers so that the chest can be taken apart if necessary, and use countersunk wood screws to attach the base/drawer unit in place. Then press the magnetic catches in place on the doors, install the catch plates in their holes and hinge the doors.

Fit the wings, vertical stretchers and back panel in position on the bottom section, and apply glue to the insides of the mortises of the top.

Turning the unit on its side, with the tenons of the vertical stretchers started in their mortises, slide each wing unit into its hole before clamping the top in place.

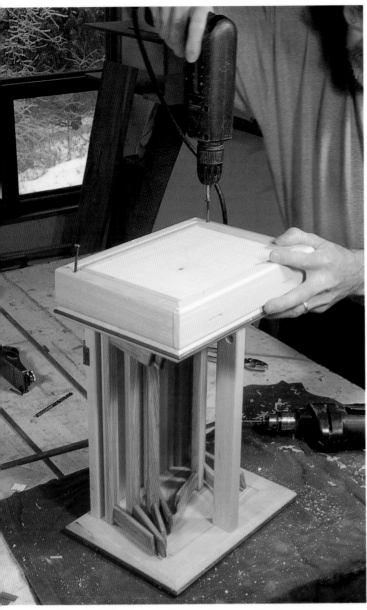

Use screws to attach the base to the assembled upper unit. Having the drawer in place allows you to adjust the base for good drawer fit as the pilot holes are drilled and the screws are tightened.

Install the doors after finishing is complete.

CHAPTER 16

Fiddleback Maple Jewelry Chest

This jewelry chest's design, with its soft, rounded edges, is more feminine than much of my work, and reminds me of the old Wurlitzer jukeboxes. When I designed this piece, I was at a two-week-long craft show, with dismal rain and cold in October and looking out from my little covered building with no potential customers in sight. After finishing up the small bits of carving I'd brought along to amuse myself in idle times, I sketched this piece on the back of a business card—which I carried in my pocket for weeks before I was able to find the right materials and the time to get started. It

is a simple piece that is difficult to make because of the number of interrelated parts and the tolerances necessary for them to work. It offers divided drawer compartments, a hinged lid compartment for rings and miscellaneous items, and opening side compartments for necklaces to be hung. This is a simple-looking project with all the complications of a large piece of furniture, and is offered here for the advanced woodworker. I suggest that a beginning woodworker learn some of the techniques used in this project by practicing on some of the simpler ones offered in this book before attempting to make this jewelry

MATERIALS LIST

Fiddleback maple

Hard maple · · · (for drawers and drawer guides)

Baltic birch plywood · · · 1/8" (for drawer bottoms, compartment bottom and back)

Plywood · · · 3/4" (for making templates)

Carcass

Vertical stretchers	4 pcs.	3/4" × 1 1/4" × 13 3/4"
Horizontal side stretchers	4 pcs.	3/4" × 1 1/2" × 7 1/2" [1]
Front stretcher	1 pc.	3/4" × 1" × 9" [2]
Back stretcher	1 pc.	3/4" × 2 1/2" × 9" [2]

Base

Front and back	2 pcs.	3/4" × 2 1/4" × 12 1/4"
Side pieces	2 pcs.	3/4" × 2 1/4" × 9 7/8"
Interior panel	1 pc.	1/8" × 5 3/4" × 8 1/8" (Baltic birch)
Back panel	1 pc.	1/8" × 8 3/8" × 11 3/8" (Baltic birch)
Interior top panel	1 pc.	1/8" × 6 7/8" × 8 3/8" (Baltic birch)
Drawer guides	12 pcs.	3/8" × 3/8" × 7"
Necklace hanger/ Compartment sides	2 pcs.	3/8" × 1 11/16" × 6 3/8"

Doors

Stiles	4 pcs.	3/4" × 1 1/4" × 13 1/4"
Bottom rails	2 pcs.	3/4" × 1 3/4" × 7" [1]
Top rails	2 pcs.	3/4" × 1 1/2" × 7" [1]
Panels	2 pcs.	1/4" × 5 15/16" × 10 23/32" (resawn from 13/16" stock)
Necklace hangers	2 pcs.	1/4" × 1 1/4" × 5 7/16"

Drawers

Bottoms	6 pcs.	7 1/2" × 7 9/16" × 1/8" (1/8" Baltic birch)
Interior dividers	6 pcs.	1/8" × 7/8" × 7 1/2"
Drawer pulls	6 pcs.	3/8" × 1 1/4" × 9/16"

Top drawers

Fronts	3 pcs.	5/16" × 1 1/2" × 8"
Sides	6 pcs.	5/16" × 1 1/2" × 7 7/8" (includes 3/16" tenon)
Backs	3 pcs.	5/16" × 1 1/2" × 7 11/16"

Middle drawers

Fronts	2 pcs.	5/16" × 2" × 8"
Sides	4 pcs.	5/16" × 2" × 7 7/8" (includes tenon)
Backs	2 pcs.	5/16" × 2" × 7 11/16"

Bottom drawer

Front	1 pc.	5/16" × 2 1/4" × 8"
Sides	2 pcs.	5/16" × 2" × 7 7/8" (includes tenon)
Back	1 pc.	5/16" × 2 1/4" × 7 11/16"

Lid

Back stretcher	1 pc.	5/8" × 1 1/8" × 8"
Sides	2 pcs.	5/8" × 1 1/8" × 5 3/4" [2]
Front	1 pc.	5/8" × 3" × 8" (shaped from stock)
Top panel	1 pc.	1/4" × 5 3/16" × 6 3/16"

Hardware

Brass pins	18 pcs.	1/8" × 5/8" (for sides)
	14 pcs.	1/8" × 1/2" (for doors)
Magnetic catches	2 pcs.	5/16" (with catch plates)
Barrel hinges	4 pcs.	12mm
	2 pcs.	10mm

[1] Measurement includes 3/4" tenons on each end.
[2] Measurement includes 1/2" tenons on each end.

chest. Many of the techniques used in making this chest are used and described elsewhere in this book, and rather than go over these again, I offer photos of the steps not previously covered and a narrative of all the steps used in completing the project.

TOOLS LIST

Table saw	Band saw
Planer	Jointer
6" × 48" belt sander	Router table
21/64" drill bit for 5/16" magnetic catches	Drill press with 10mm and 12mm boring bits
1/8" brad-point drill bit	Various bits

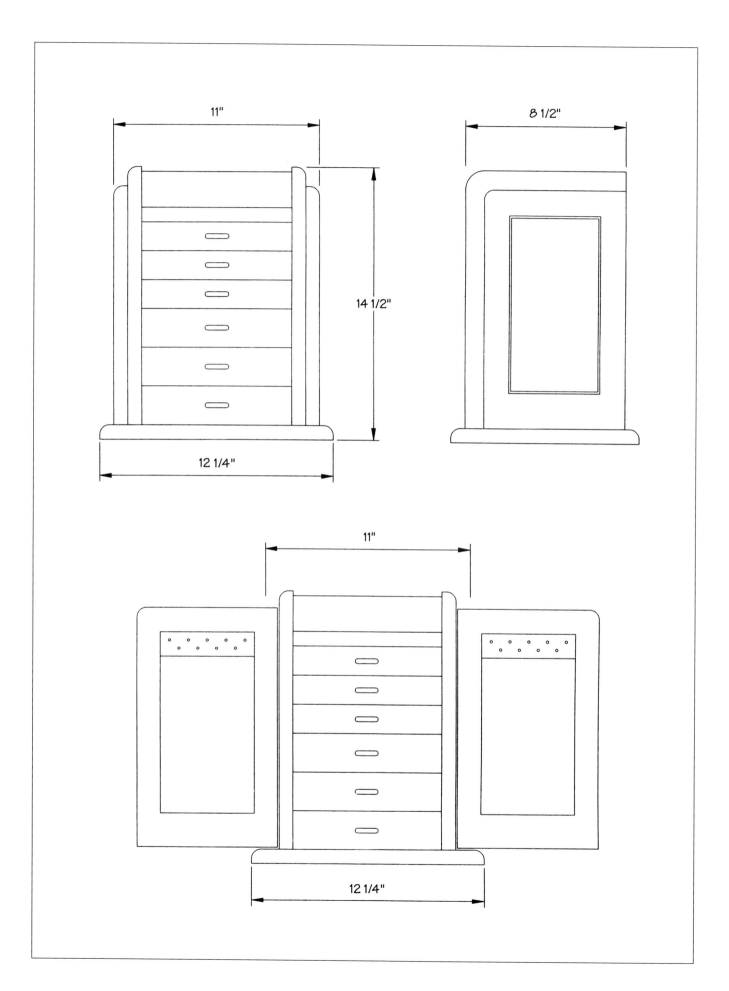

MAKING THE JEWELRY CHEST

STEP 1
Make the Door Panels

Resaw the material for the door panels on the band saw and surface it to ¼" thick. Because of the intense figure of fiddleback maple and its tendency to tear-out, run the panels through a thickness sander. This operation can be done with the planer, but use a freshly sharpened set of knives to avoid tear-out. I used the thickness sander for dimensioning all the stock for this project to avoid the loss—and waste—of expensive material.

STEP 2
Cut All of the Frame Parts

Cut all the parts of the interior frames and the door frame parts to dimension, and route the mortises in the vertical stretchers. Then cut the tenons on the ends of the door rails and the rails of the interior frames.

STEP 3
Assemble the Door Frames

Assemble the door frames and interior frames to chamfer the inside edges, and use the straight chisel to finish the corners as in making the door frames for Rachel's jewelry cabinet (see chapter fourteen).

STEP 4
Make the Lid

Make the curved front piece of the lid by gluing angled stock cut from a wider piece. Try to keep the pieces in sequence so that the grain will match as closely as possible. (The photos at right top and center show the process used.)

Use an old cabinet scraper with a corner ground to about a ³⁄₁₆" radius to scrape out the excess glue and form a small cove on the inside corner. To shape this piece to a smooth radius, use the 6" × 48" belt sander. Use this piece as the basis for determining the profiles of the top front corners of the interior frames and the doors.

STEP 5
Make the Necklace Hangers

Before assembling the interior frames, make necklace hangers, which also serve as sides for the interior of the top compartment. I use the Shop Smith as a drill press, with the table at a 15° angle, to drill holes for the brass pins to fit. In order for these pieces to fit in the frames, use a ⅛" straight-cut router bit to cut slots in the front,

The front stretcher of the lid is formed from three pieces of fiddleback maple. Put tape on the face side while the three pieces are held together. Then open the parts up at the back, with the tape acting as a hinge. With glue in place, tape the parts across the inside, spreading the glue and pulling the tape tight to hold the joint tight while the glue sets.

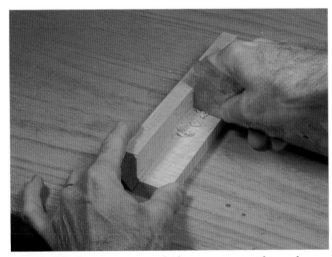

Use an old cabinet scraper with the corner ground round to clean out the excess glue and form the inside cove.

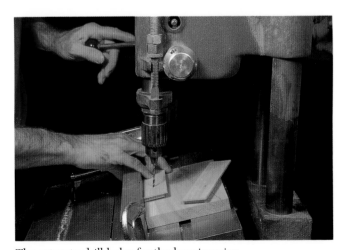

The setup to drill holes for the hanging pins.

back and top pieces of the frames. For the front and back pieces, set up stop blocks to control the length and location of the slots, and cut them ³⁄₁₆″ deep. Use a ¾″ straight-cut router bit to cut the tongues on three sides of the hanger pieces, and cut a ⅛″ saw kerf, ⅛″ deep, on the opposite side from the holes for the bottom panel of the top compartment to fit. Also, route a small chamfer on the outside bottom edge of these pieces. After sanding the necklace hanger pieces, the interior frames are ready to assemble.

STEP 6
Trim Cut Tongues on the Door Panels

Cut the door panels to size, allowing about ¹⁄₁₆″ of expansion space and ¹⁄₃₂″ clearance in length, and add ½″ to each dimension over the interior dimensions of the door frames. Cut tongues on the panels ⅛″ thick × ¼″ using the technique used to form the panels for the doors for Rachel's jewelry cabinet. Very lightly chamfer the insides of the door frames and route a matching chamfer in the door panels. Sand the inside edges of the chamfer on the door frames and sand the panels inside and out before assembly.

STEP 7
Assemble the Interior Panels

It is very important to check the interior panels for square as they are assembled, as this can affect the accuracy of the routing to install the drawer guides.

STEP 8
Cut the Drawer Guide Slots in the Interior Frames

Use the plunge router and fence to make the guide jig for cutting the drawer guide slots in the interior frames. Route ⅝″ slots through the template for the interior frames, with the center lines spaced to correspond with the center lines of the intended drawer guide locations. With my router and fence setup, I am only able to use the fence to reach the first two, and then must rely on clamped-on fences for the router to follow in making its cut for the last four. Use a ⅜″ carbide spiral cutter in the router, along with a ⅝″ guide bushing, to follow the routed slots in the template. Mark the interior frames for left and right, and turn the template over when routing the opposite side to avoid problems that might come from inaccuracy in routing the slots.

Cut mortises in the interior frame parts for the necklace hanger to fit. Using a ⅛″ straight-cut bit, use stop blocks to control the length of cut and relocate the stop blocks for routing the opposite side.

Assemble the interior framework of the jewelry chest with glue squeezed into the mortises. After clamping, check that the frames are square.

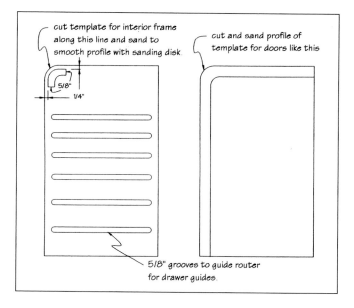

cut template for interior frame along this line and sand to smooth profile with sanding disk.

cut and sand profile of template for doors like this

5/8″   1/4″

5/8″ grooves to guide router for drawer guides.

Use a template and the guide bushing in the router base for the drawer guides to fit. Turn the template over to route the opposite side. I have this same template profiled on the the front top corner for marking and routing the interior frames later. This helps me to be certain that I am using it the right way on the opposite sides.

To make the drawer guides, tape a number of them together to route at the same time. Using a ³⁄₁₆″ roundover allows them to fit into the ³⁄₈″ slots routed for them in the interior frames. Taping them together allows me to get a cleaner, safer and faster operation. Slide a block along at the back side to hold them evenly against the fence and guide bearing of the router bit.

Do the final shaping of the drawer guides with a straight cutter in the router table. Take a little off each side, making the part that will slide into the channel on the drawer sides just under ¼″ wide.

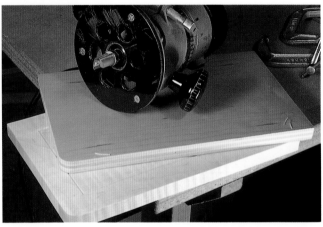

Use the router, template and template-following router bit to route the top front corners of the doors to their finished profile. The doors and interior frames are done in the same way, but require different templates. Use the band saw to cut away some of the waste at the corners before routing to get a cleaner cut.

STEP 9
Make and Install the Drawer Guides

To make the drawer guides, use masking tape to hold the pieces together for accurate and safe milling. Using the ³⁄₁₆″ roundover on the end allows it to fit the ³⁄₈″ routed slots in the frames. In order for the drawer guides to fit into ¼″ slots on the sides of the drawers, use a straight-cut bit to take off a bit from each side, reducing the width on the inner surface to just less than ¼″. Set the height of the cut so that the shoulder of the ³⁄₈″ portion will be flush with the inside surfaces of the frame when in place. Drill ⅛″ holes near the ends of each drawer guide so that they can be held in place with ⅛″ dowel pins.

STEP 10
Route Mortises for the Cross Stretchers

Before installing the drawer guides, route mortises for the tenoned cross stretchers to fit: These mortises are ½″ deep and vary in length and position between the front and back of the frames. Use a ³⁄₈″ bit in the plunge router, and route between pencil lines drawn in place with a square. Next, plunge the bit into the work and move the router back and forth between the lines until it reaches the right depth. Next route the ⅛″ dadoes in the back edges of the frames for the back panel to fit. Change the location of the stop block for the left and right sides.

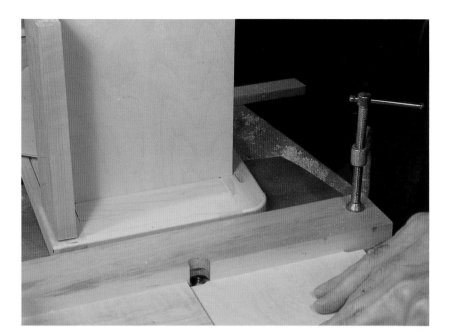

In order for the bottom of the top compartment to fit into the dadoes cut for it in the sides and front and back stretchers, make a small relief cut with a straight-cut router bit.

Use the drill press to drill the holes for the barrel hinges to fit the interior frames and doors.

STEP 11
Make the Cross Stretchers
Form the tenoned cross stretchers for the front and back in the usual way, then cut ⅛" dadoes along their bottom edges for the bottom panel of the top compartment to fit.

STEP 12
Shape the Doors and Interior Frames
To shape the profiles of the door panels and interior frames, lay the template in place, trace the outline of the curved corner on the assembled piece and make a preliminary cut with the band saw, cutting just barely outside the line. This allows you to take a very slight cut with the template-following bit in the router, reducing the chance of tear-out.

STEP 13
Make the Bottom of the Cabinet
Make the bottom of the cabinet with ¾" × 2¼" stock and use #20 biscuits to join the mitered corners. Install the biscuits close to the inside of the miter to keep them from being revealed when the corners are routed to shape.

Cut a ⅛" × ¼" slot around the inside of the parts, offset to avoid interfering with the centered biscuits, for the ⅛" Baltic birch plywood to fit. Chamfer the inside edges of the parts, sand the inside edges and the bottom panel, and then assemble this unit in the same manner as the top and bottom of the earring chest. Route a ⅛" dado across the back of the base unit for the back panel to fit, and use the technique used in shaping the top corners of the doors and interior dividers to give the bottom unit its curved

To transfer the setting to accurately drill the other side, drill a hole in a piece of scrap using the first setting. By turning the piece over, you can use it to position the stop block for the matching hole. At this point, you are most interested in getting the holes to match, and will provide clearance for the doors to swing in a later operation.

corners. To prepare the bottom of the top compartment to fit, trim the corners to give clearance to the inside surfaces of the interior frames.

To prepare the interior frames for hanging the doors, follow the procedure, shown in the photos, for both the frames and doors. In order to use the magnetic catches, they must have their holes drilled before assembly.

STEP 14
Install the Drawer Guides

When these operations are complete, and the routing of contours and sanding of the interior panels is complete, install the drawer guides. After the drawer guides are in place, sand off the little nubs of the ⅛″ dowels left standing, and lightly sand the edges of the drawer guides with a sanding block.

STEP 15
Drill the Holes for the Lid Hinges

The last steps in getting ready to assemble the jewelry chest are to drill for the 10mm barrel hinges to fit the back cross stretcher and lid, to route the cross stretchers with a ⅛″ roundover on the outside edges and a ¹⁄₁₆″ roundover on the inside edges and to sand. To drill for the barrel hinges, use the techniques used for the doors and interior frames, except use ⅛″ plywood for the stop blocks on the drill press so that the tenons on the back cross stretcher do not interfere with positioning the workpiece.

STEP 16
Assemble the Chest

To assemble the jewelry chest, use glue in the mortises, and clamps with cushion blocks to pull the joints tight. Be

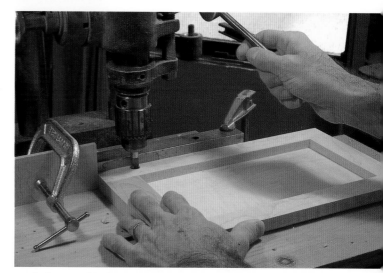

With the stop block repositioned, you can drill the matching hole.

very careful at this point to check that the assembly is square, and to check to make certain that the distance from the bottom edge of the frame to the bottom edges of the cross stretchers is equal at all four corners.

STEP 17
Make the Drawers

Make the drawers with mortise-and-tenon joints, using mortises in the drawer fronts to connect with tenons on the sides, and mortises at the back corners of the sides to connect with tenons on the backs. Use dividers in the top three drawers, with the bottom drawers left open for larger items. Make the drawers using the techniques outlined earlier in the book. Cut the drawer fronts exactly the same width as the inside of the chest, knowing that sanding away a small cleanup allowance will give me a good fit.

ATTENTION AND MEDITATION

Woodworking can be a dangerous occupation or hobby. The high level of attention it requires precludes working when angry or preoccupied with outside the shop matters. I learned this the hard way, by dadoing my thumb while finishing a small project the day before getting married. It is important to me that my shop be a place of peace, allowing me to focus my attention directly on the task at hand. I've found this to be the only safe way to work, and infinitely rewarding. I believe the thing that engages so many people in woodworking is what meditation teachers call mindfulness. Many of us have entered a timeless space in our workshops and in our work, in which we have been so engaged by the processes of making things that we take no note of time passing, and are at last awakened to external consciousness by the words, "Aren't you coming to bed?" Even after twenty years, woodworking can do that to me. For beginning woodworkers, the excitement of learning new things empowers our ability to focus undisturbed attention on processes happening at our fingertips. By pursuing the development of new skills and practicing new techniques, by developing new designs, and acquiring new tools and learning their use, we gain the energy required to focus our attention from our enthusiasm. In addition, the ability to focus your attention grows through regular practice like every other human activity. I have come to believe, through watching the various relationships involved in my woodworking activities, that there is actually a lot more going on than meets the eye, that would be described as coincidental or spiritual, depending on your particular perspective. An artist friend of mine, Louis Freund, explains that the artist's work is essentially spiritual in nature, as we create work that has never been seen before, risking censorship and failure while guided by our own inner vision. For me, meditation is a way to integrate all the complex relationships of woodworking into a single vision. I practice two forms of meditation: one that could be called "sitting" meditation, and a second, "active" meditation, the practice of "dual awareness." Sitting meditation is a way to gain composure and focus. I find it very useful to "sit" in a comfortable position for a few minutes each day. I meditate to get clear and focused on who I am and what I'm doing, keeping in mind that I may not be here to change the world, and that my working with wood may as well be the way in which I myself am changed. In practicing dual awareness, I simply proceed with the task at hand, but with my attention divided between a focus on inner purpose and on what my hands are doing. It is good to begin practicing this on some of the less dangerous jobs in the shop. After a while it becomes an almost automatic way of working. As you practice this meditation, you may begin to actually sense the downward response in energy flow that comes from contact with inner purpose. For me, part of the challenge of being a woodworker is maintaining a connection to higher purpose. I am personally not satisfied with making "stuff." The world is already full of meaningless things that satisfy some immediate needs but are quickly hustled off to fill landfills. I have hopes that my work can awaken, and inform, while expressing caring and concern for our natural world. We work within the context of a tradition going back thousands of years to the first mortise-and-tenon joint. We work with woods grown in forests that are thousands of years old. We work in a time of human history when basic human values seem confused, and when our unreasoned misuse of the Earth's resources must be questioned. Meditation helps me to reconcile these factors and move toward what I believe to be good works. Human beings are unique among the inhabitants of our planet in that we have choices in our sense of self. It is like television in that we can identify with a variety of self-images in the same way one can watch a variety of channels. We can perceive of ourselves as purely physical beings concerned with fulfilling physical needs; emotional beings concerned with pleasing other people to gain emotional support and acknowledgement; mental beings wrestling with intellectual concepts; or spiritual beings connected with others through these means and more. A normal human being is continually shifting focus or "channel surfing" throughout the day. Meditation is a means by which I can make an effort to observe myself and begin reconciling all the various aspects of being human. While, for some, the woodworking shop may be a retreat from the concerns of the world and a place to recharge the spirit before reentering the workplace, mine has become a place through which I connect with the world, try to learn from it, and hopefully reconnect with and share human values that appear in some ways to be endangered.

STEP 18

Fit the Drawer Guides

To fit the drawers to the drawer guides, first route test pieces and check their actual fit in the jewelry chest. Once you are satisfied with the fit of the drawer sides, keep them in order and assemble the drawers, being careful to check that they are square and lay flat on the bench. After the drawers are complete, route for the drawer pulls to fit, using the ⅛″ straight-cut router bit, with the fence and stop blocks to position the mortise slightly above the center of each drawer. Route the top and bottom edges of the drawer front on each drawer with a ⅛″ roundover bit—except the bottom drawer, which you should leave straight on the bottom to look right against the bottom of the chest.

STEP 19

Attach the Upper Assembly to the Base

Use countersunk wood screws to attach the upper assembly to the base, and use a piece of plywood in the bottom during assembly to make certain that the unit is square and equal in width to the upper portion. In fitting the doors and lid of the upper compartment, use the tapered sanding disk and cutoff box in the table saw to sand about ⅟₃₂″ at the bottom of the doors and ⅟₃₂″ from each side of the assembled lid to give clearance for opening.

STEP 20

Finishing and Installing the Doors and Lid

Apply the oil finish to the chest before installing the doors and lid to avoid getting oil on the hinge mechanism, which could cause the doors and lid to become difficult to open and close and cause unnecessary wear.

Route test pieces to check the router settings and clearances between drawers as you route the drawer sides to fit the drawer guides.

With the drawer sides fitted to the drawer guides, assemble the drawers. Number the drawers from top to bottom to be certain that they go back in the correct spots.

Using clamps to hold the parts in place, drill and countersink the screw holes, then install the screws, securing the bottom to the framework of the chest.

SOURCES OF SUPPLIES

Woodcraft Supply
210 Wood County Industrial Park
P.O. Box 1686
Parkersville, WV 26102-1686
Phone (800) 225-1153
Hardware and hand tools.

Jesada Tools
310 Mears Blvd.
P.O. Box 1518
Oldsmar, FL 34677
Phone (800) 531-5559
Cutting tools.

Klingspors' Sanding Catalog
P.O. Box 5069
Hickory, NC 28603-5069
Phone (800) 228-0000
Abrasives.

INDEX